Secrets of a Telephone Psychic

Secrets of a Telephone Psychic

Frederick Woodruff

Beyond Words Publishing, Inc.
20827 N.W. Cornell Road, Suite 500
Hillsboro, Oregon 97124-9808
503-531-8700
1-800-284-9673

The publisher and author gratefully acknowledge permission to use the excerpts on pages 31 and 44 from "Ask Camille." This article first appeared in *Salon*, an online magazine, at *http://www.salonmagazine.com*. Reprinted with permission.

The names and locations featured in this book are fictitious. To prevent legal complications due to the restraints of contracts that the author was required to sign in order to don a psychic-line headset, all events "retold" within these pages are culled from an amalgam of telephone conversations and personal, face-to-face counseling sessions. In other words, they are name-changed composite characters reconjured from the burning pit of the author's memory and reassembled for your enjoyment and, hopefully, enlightenment.

Editor: Sheryl Fullerton
Proofreader: Marvin Moore
Design: Eric Nord and Frederick Woodruff
Composition: William H. Brunson Typography Services
Managing editor: Kathy Matthews

Printed in the United States of America
Distributed to the book trade by Publishers Group West

Library of Congress Cataloging-in-Publication Data
Woodruff, Frederick, 1956–
Secrets of a telephone psychic / Frederick Woodruff.
p. cm.
Includes bibliographical references.
ISBN 1-885223-89-7 (pbk.)
1. Psychics—United States. 2. Audiotex services industry—United States. I. Title.
BF1040.W74 1998
133.8—dc21 98-35780
CIP

The corporate mission of Beyond Words Publishing, Inc.:
Inspire to Integrity

Contents

Dial Tone: An Introduction

In the middle of the road of my life
I awoke in a dark wood where the true way was wholly lost.
DANTE

"Good-bye." *Click.*

I swill some water and clear my occupationally-hazarded throat. I figure I've got about sixty seconds of sweet silence before the next call. I began my "shift" around ten this morning. It's now almost eleven and already the neurons in my head feel like automatic-weapons fire of an angry mob. For the last hour I have been inundated by a whirlwind of clashing voices from America's Pandora's toy-box of dashed hopes, dilapidated dreams, debilitated romances, and derailed schemes—sprinkled throughout with the garden-variety requests for lost car keys and pregnancy diagnostics. But that last call was "a keeper," meaning I jot down a quick note in my log book to remind myself of the conversation's content. It reads: "10:50 A.M.: Guy wanted to know if I knew anything about Princess Di's whereabouts on the astral plane. He sounded like Robert Blake."

I told him I didn't make it a habit to disturb the deceased, and he retorted that I should brush up on my séance skills.

"People are paying $3.99 a minute for this service ya know."

And then he challenged me: "That old guy on the other psychic infomercial talks to Marilyn Monroe all of the time. If he can do that why can't you tell me some stuff about Diana?"

I rolled my eyes and said, "Because 'that old guy' representing that other psychic network thinks he *is* Marilyn Monroe." A short pause and then I add, "Something strange has happened to his clairvoyant circuitry. It's a bad neocortex misfire. It's like he's reading into *himself*. In the psychic biz we classify that as SGCWIS, or, self-generated circumnavigational walk-in syndrome."

My sarcasm didn't even register as the caller plowed forward.

"Well, I still would like to know if Diana is in a safe place," he persisted. "So what's the number for that other psychic network?"

And that's when I said good-bye. I don't have that number. And I don't have Marilyn's *or* Lady Di's either. Sorry.

My Plantronics PLX-400 telephone and headset seems to shimmy a little when the next call comes in.

"Hi. This is Frederick, and thanks for calling the psy . . ."

"Hello? Hello! I'm premenstrual . . ." The voice on the other end is taut, almost out of breath, and there's a rhythmic grinding sound coming from the background.

In my electronic world, the voice is a second face. But lately I've come to envision the whole body—head to toe—and in this case it's a good-sized woman wearing lots of lipstick and sporting a troubled perm, imbibing her second cup of coffee, while working up a frenzy on her Stairmaster. I try to finish my greeting, the one the company I work for requires. But she's determined to present her case.

"Does that matter, I mean, to do the reading properly? I thought maybe the PMS thing might disturb the vibrations or something. You know, the frequencies in the reading. So, can you read me, because, you know, like I said I'm premenstrual?"

"Well," I think to myself, "I'm *postmodern*! Just look at my job."

Imagine turning forty and you've just landed a job as a telephone psychic. When I reluctantly told a few of my friends (the kind of friends you can actually trust with a secret) that I was a bona fide—*real, live*—psychic pal, I was prepared for some derisive feedback.

"Look, I'm having an out-of-money experience, so I took a job working for one of those big 900 psychic networks," I sheepishly explained.

My friend Vedika thought it was charming.

I wasn't so sure. I'd envisioned myself at forty doing so much more: an accomplished artist, published writer, or at least managing my own Wendy's. But phone psychic? It wasn't exactly the opportunity of a lifetime to work in a business that was routinely, at different times throughout the decade, hawked on post-midnight television by just about every last remaining member of the Love Boat.

Always a bit of a Zen-like advisor, Vedika countered my discomfort. "See what you can learn from the experience. Just go with it for a while. Something is going to be revealed here," she said. "What's your problem with it exactly?"

I had spent years as a professional astrologer and tarot specialist. I thought my objection should be obvious. "Look, me on a psychic hot line is like Dr. Christiaan Barnard answering calls for Dial-a-Nurse. I'm overqualified, don'tcha think?"

"Sounds like a little bit of hubris to me. Consider it this way: like you've taken a vow of service, to all humankind. You know, a Bodhisattva sort of thing," she offered.

I laughed, but then, a month later, after fielding my umpteenth call, that's exactly what I did. Her suggestion quelled my damaged self-image. And she was right. The array of insights I gleaned from the hearts and minds of a wild cross-section of Americans was enough to send a Gallup pollster into a swoon.

I tried my newfound rationale out on my spiritual teacher, Morton.

"It's like talking and listening to pop culture's collective unconscious," I was explaining to him on the phone one day, trying to sound like a Jungian analyst. "You know, it's like I've taken a Bodhisattva vow."

He paused for a heartbeat and then added in his Morton-does-mordant voice, "Yes, it does. A bad one."

But you know how you can find yourself involved with a seemingly insignificant event that completely transforms your life, rearranging your perspective, your idea about yourself, your relationship with your fellow human beings—your very relationship with the cosmos itself?

Well, that's not what happened here.

But it's come close, very close—in myriad ways that I am still trying to decipher and properly value. While working the phones, some amazing and shocking revelations have transpired, some heartfelt and humbling exchanges have occurred, and that's why I've written this story. And look, just picking up this tome has afforded you a significant shift in *your* life; in the last three minutes you've actually *read* the introduction to a book. Congratulations and hello—we're on our way to a good connection already.

Oh! And the premenstrual lady? We hit if off splendidly.

"Yes. I can do premenstrual," I assured her. "But postmortem is out. I just don't go there."

"What do you mean?" she asked. And I could tell she was sincere.

"Well, people call wanting to know how folks like Jimmy Stewart or Kurt Cobain or Princess Diana are doing in heaven."

"Really? That's sort of strange. But I suppose it's the nature of the business you're in."

"Tell me about it." I sneak another gulp of water.

"So the PMS thing isn't going to be a problem? I'm new to this psychic stuff, and thought I'd better ask."

"No, no problem," I say. "So what sort of topic would you like to explore today? What's on your mind? How can I help?"

"I've got several different questions about my job and my love life. I guess the thing with my boyfriend is what I'd like to talk about the most. But before we start, can I ask—how *is* Princess Diana doing?"

PART ONE

My Day and How It Got That Way

1

Gossip: The Soul of Conversation

I'm very busy finding out what people mean by what they say.
GERTRUDE STEIN

It's a little after two o'clock, and I'm sitting at my desk again. It's a slow afternoon on the phones. Calls come in one of two patterns: like a slow-moving inchworm, with long pauses between lunges; or like a cloudburst of locust—chewing and short-circuiting all the wires from the Eastern to the Western seaboards. Suddenly everyone, everywhere has just got to know if their boyfriend/girlfriend is being unfaithful. And I mean everyone. Synchronized queries like this prove over and over again how our culture, just like an individual, has undulating moods and temperaments. These waves or cycles have become so recognizable that, once noted, I'm tempted to just answer the phone with "Yes, the bastard is cheating on you. Get out of the relationship now." But instead it's "Hello! Thanks for calling the psychic network."

I moved from Honolulu to Seattle a little over a year ago. People told me I'd lost my mind, abandoning paradise for the Pacific Northwest's drizzle-fest. But after twenty years of interminable sunshine I was crying for want of a good squall of rain. Some pittance of seasonal shifting. Some leaves falling. I was ready to return to the mainland and reality. And so I did, and here I sit.

The view from my desk, in my office, in our second-floor apartment, overlooks the street and other timeworn buildings. As apartment people are apt to do, many of us watch each other, askance, through the course of the day and night. After a while we develop a silent rapport with one another. Oh, there's the woman who likes to put on old Motown records and boogie in her living room for aerobic stimulation. And there's that bald man at his computer again, staring at the monitor like it's talking to him. And of course all of those tenants are watching me with my headset in place and hands gesticulating wildly. Or, when the phones are dead and I'm chewing yet another hangnail into oblivion—and feeling lonely—I at least *hope* they are watching.

I've set up a small workspace in my office, which doubles as a bedroom. The arrangement of objects on my desk is more like an altar than a utilitarian space. It's a strange combination of electronica and esoterica. A Macintosh computer, humming alongside a glowing votive candle lit in honor of the BVM (Blessed Virgin Mary). Next to some unpaid bills are my phone logs and diary stacked on top of a slew of astrological tables, notes on a new tarot layout, and a book I consult often while counseling my callers: Marianne Williamson's *Illuminata: A Return to Prayer*. The book is dog-eared and stuffed with a fan of jutting sticky notes that make access to certain chapters quick. They read: "Substance addiction." "Prayer for attracting love." "Internal abundance creates external abundance." "Prayer for sustaining friendship." "Incarcerated spouse."

At my desk/altar, I have my agent Sheryl's latest notes regarding a book proposal that she just returned to me—the proposal that eventually became the book you are reading right now. She notes, carefully and concisely in one of the margins—with an underline: "You're talking to America every day and you've taken the patient's pulse. Now tell us the prognosis—what's it all about?"

I furrow my brow and think, "Does she realize the implications of her request?" Then I recall author Iris Murdoch's axiom: "Every book is the wreck of a perfect idea." Originally I'd intended this book to be a brainless, lighthearted recounting of my days on the psychic lines, a flick-of-the-wrist sort of creation—but now Sheryl is creating an opportunity for an actual book, something of substance and, God forbid, possible import. She's looking for some sociological analysis, hell, semiotics even. Can I do it? My brain whirs and then grinds and smokes.

I've been working like this for months: Brainstorming on this book, eating Stag chili for lunch and answering the psychic lines in between another mouthful of beans. I feel stuck, so I close my eyes and let my mind go into free-fall—a sure way for me to hit the right note as an author tackling the difficult task of opening a first paragraph or chapter or feeble couplings of words in a prayer to *counter* writer's block.

I opt for the prayer. Suddenly I'm thinking of Marianne Williamson again. I'm recalling how she used to be a cocktail-lounge singer and now she is the supreme channeler for the *Course in Miracles* philosophies. That was one hell of a career leap. What would Marianne suggest? "Just pray," she'd say. So, yes, that's what I'll do. My prayer, like most prayers, begins by highlighting a dilemma, some discomfort, and it goes like this:

> *Dear Creator or Creatoress of the Universe:*
>
> *I have landed in what the pundits of popular culture deem the "circle of outside artists." We are a group of unfortunate souls isolated by circumstance from mainstream society and yet not daunted from creating our gifts. I too have become secluded from my fellow humankind, working at home, alone, diligently, on a psychic hot line, in attempts to pay the rent and buy new underwear. Although I am trapped in my bedroom/office, yacking for hours on end with a telephone headset strapped to my skull, all hope is not lost. I gather strength in remembering other outsiders who excelled in their craft despite their circumstances. Recognizable literary giants like Emily Dickinson and Marcel Proust come immediately to mind. But, as a writer* and *a visual artist, I prefer to consider the more obscure painters from our century. I only have to recall how Raymond Masterson, while serving a protracted prison term, began to make minute embroideries*

using colored thread from his tube socks, or how my most inspiring hero, Martin Ramirez, spent most of his life in a mental institution creating intricate drawings on discarded pieces of paper pasted together with a glue made out of potatoes and his very own saliva. From a more contemporary angle there's Latoya Jackson, who, well, never mind, she's presently suing the psychic line that "leased" her image.

I too have a cache of material to work with: my wellspring of stories, anecdotes, secrets, and gossip—lots of it to tell and weave into a recounting the likes of which has not been seen since Roger Ebert's screenplay for Beyond the Valley of the Dolls. *So, my entreatment to you, O Omnipotent One, is for guidance, illumination, and the patience to endure with grace and humor.*

Oh, and my final request is simple: Despite my appreciation for Jenny Jones (another outsider, who in her early days was arrested by the police and incarcerated on different occasions), please, let me meet Oprah Winfrey first. Thank you.

Your humble servant and electronic messenger, Frederick

It's fitting to open the first chapter in a book about telephone psychics with a prayer. This mirrors the attitude of the people who call me. Hope is a high commodity; without it the companies that run psychic networks would go broke. And right after hope—and humankind's ability to generate endless supplies of it—comes the need to gossip.

As the poet W. H. Auden told a radio interviewer, "Gossip is the art-form of the man and woman in the street, and the proper subject for gossip, as for all art, is the behavior of mankind." Now, in my line of business, the man and woman in the street is, indeed, every one of us—not only the plebeian but the men and women who live up on the hill. *Everyone* calls psychics: housewives, students, CEOs, doctors, nurses, prisoners—well, spouses of prisoners, although I did take a conference call once from a woman *and* her incarcerated husband. The consultation was unnerving. I was a novice, and this arrangement was the first time I realized how bizarre this job was going to be. The woman's name was Tara and her boyfriend's name was Jimmy Jack, and the conversation went like this:

"So we really need to see what is gonna be our future together. How this relationship is gonna work. What we can look forward to," Tara requested.

I shuffled the cards and laid them carefully in front of me. The picture wasn't looking too good. In fact, it was downright depressing. But then what did I expect? Jimmy Jack, who had the proverbial record as long as his arm, was in jail for nearly killing Tara's former lover.

"I feel like I need to be frank about this. The cards indicate some difficult challenges for the two of you," I cautiously offered.

"Well what in the hell do ya expect. I'm in jail," yelled Jimmy Jack.

"I understand that. But Tara was telling me that there were problems between the two of you before you even went to jail. Is that true?"

"Hey, you're the psychic. Do I really need to answer that, Tara? This seems like a waste of money. Do I need to answer that? How much are you paying for this goddamned shit?"

"Jimmy J, let him talk about this stuff, 'cause you gotta lotta time to think about whatever he is gonna tell us." And then Tara prompted me to continue.

"What exactly is your sentence?" I asked. "How long are you in for?"

"Ten to twelve more years," Jimmy Jack growled.

The spray of tarot cards in front of me went blank, their bright hues and quirky illustrations looked cryptic and suddenly unfamiliar. I was accustomed to providing readings for people who were free to walk the sidewalks of America and contemplate new jobs or relationships or the consequences of robbing a bank. What do you tell a couple who *already* know what the future holds for them? The best way to bake a file into a cake? Well, as it turned out, I didn't need to say much. Instead I sat back and just listened—to their complaints, their accusations, their stories—the secrets and confessions. The gossip.

That was the first time I realized that we talk, yack, tell fish tales, swap rumors, and gossip as a way to soothe our concern with the present and our apprehension about the future. Something magical happens when we move our mouth and utter words about ourselves, about others. Talking is a seemingly innocuous act, but cogent and transformative, as psychologists can attest with their "talking cures."

I think etymologies offer clues that we can follow to apprehend the secret of any given object or event. Not surprisingly, the word *gossip* has a strange history. Originally, as a noun, it meant "god-relative" or a "close friend." As a telephone psychic, this is what I have to offer my callers. I'm an invisible friend with a supposed connection to higher forces or powers. And I'm all ears.

As a writer, I'm all mouth, and I've written this book in the same garrulous spirit. This will be a friendly rapport that involves secrets, chatter, facts, fantasies, anecdotes, small *and* big talk—the quotidian and the metaphysical—and everything else in between. And, of course, gossip. I'm certain this book became fuel for my editor's checklist of reasons to abandon the business because it's so discursive and non sequitur riddled—but then, that's the charm of gossip and the disturbing, sometimes tacky inquisitiveness of human beings. One minute we're discussing Roseanne's recent liposuction surgery and the next we're trying to track down the 800 number that lets us bid on bits of exploded fuselage from the latest airline tragedy.

Gossip's Soothing Balm

As a kid I couldn't watch enough of the roller derby on television—especially the Thunderbirds' female division. I grew up in a home environment that was dominated by women. I shuttled between living with my divorced mom, my grandmother, and my aunt, and visiting and then finally living with my stepmom and dad. The female roller derby, with its staged brawls, cat scratching, and fist fighting, was an excellent vent for the suppressed subterfuge and hostility that charged the matriarchal air in my family. As an adult I feel the same way about the World Federation of Wrestling, monster truck and crash car derbies, gangster rap lyrics, and pornography on the Internet. And gossip. All of these pastimes are goofy vehicles for us to safely discharge our repressed rage or libidinal longings. As Auden noted in that same radio show, "When one reads in the papers of some unfortunate man who has gone for his wife with a razor, one can be pretty certain that he wasn't a great gossip."

Aside from its purgative qualities, and more essentially, gossip is the true soul of conversation. We're embarrassed that we enjoy it, but the truth is that gossip feels good. It's fun. It brings out the raconteur in each of us. The information age is nothing more than a by-product of our ardor for specific and colorful details. I love discovering things like when and where ketchup was invented, or who devised the first set of ball bearings and why, and what they were wearing when they did it. Think about it: If you had to choose between the serious study and the amusing gossip, say between Stefan Sharff's *The Elements of Cinema* and Kenneth Anger's *Hollywood Babylon,* wouldn't you choose the latter? Who would rather learn the facts of Errol Flynn's philosophy about acting than discover that he was a wanton sex machine with a bad case of halitosis?

People want details. They want to hear intimate stories about other people. And through psychic feedback, they want to hear intimate stories about *themselves.* And even more urgently, they want to talk about other people. Gossiping about significant others, rolling-pin-toting wives, rambunctious teenagers, the tartish neighbor down the street—these subjects make up the bulk of conversations on the lines. And this is one of the main reasons people call telephone psychics. This is also why people want to know what it's like *being* a telephone psychic.

So, people ask me pointed and personal questions when they call: "Where do you live? Are you married or single? Gay or straight? Cute or ugly?" And then finally, "Are you really psychic? How do you do it? Where do you do it? What do you *wear* when you're doing it?" This is how books like this are written. Questions beg answers. Vivid details. So, many questions will be answered for you throughout this book. Astounding tales will be told. And gossip and secrets *will* be revealed.

As for what I wear, well, to be perfectly frank, most of the time I'm barely dressed. The rune makers of the Teutons and Vikings wore startling garb that made them stand out in a crowd. Aboriginal shamans cover their bodies in ash. I don't know what ancient cult capitalized on the turban and bangle-earrings ensemble. But I'm usually in my underwear, especially during the summer months. That bald guy who lives in the apartment building across the street from me gets a peculiar view every morning—a nearly nude male, drinking coffee, shifting around in a chair, shuffling cards, and sporting a telephone headset. He's got to wonder, "What in the hell is *that* guy's job?" Maybe he thinks I'm a bookie or commodities trader, what with all the shuffling of cards and papers. I guess in a way I *am* working with futures—just not hog bellies and soybeans.

My lack of attire is one of the conveniences associated with a job where the customer can't see what you are doing. I sit here, disheveled and dazed, behind my desk/altar with stacks of tarot cards and astrological charts fanned before me. Alongside my phone, a bottle of Advil acts as a friendly talisman. And here we go: Soon the ringing begins. My headset is in place and ready to receive all of those fiber-optic transmissions from the roiling heart and mind of America. This is the start of my workday—another day in the life of a telephone psychic.

2
The "F" Word

The future isn't what it used to be.
YOGI BERRA

What about the future?

More global warming, presidential sexcapades, overstuffed landfills, the recurrent Super Bowl. Mother Nature's water breaks and there's another flood in Missouri, a mudslide in Malibu. The notion of "the future," when we stop and consider it, feels like something "out there," removed from us, something we are safe from. No biggie; let someone else worry about it.

But what about *your* future?

That puts a different spin on it, doesn't it? Now, suppose I tell you that I can take a peek into that place, "your future," wherever it might reside? Let's say I'll rummage around a little and come up with some pertinent details? Oh, here's something intriguing about an upcoming speed bump on the road of your relationship with your spouse. And, uh oh, that situation with your new boss looks challenging. Conversely, I'm pleased to say that all of those roses you planted will bloom this spring and might even win you an award of some kind—at least some praise from your mother-in-law. And your overall financial situation? Should you dip into that stash of loot in your Christmas club? Should you buy that new Honda Accord? Should you play the lottery or should you just stay on welfare? And what about the seemingly insignificant quandries we find ourselves considering? Those Olestra potato chips—will you or will you not develop stomach cramping and loose stools? The list of anxieties and questions is quite long. And answers few—and expensive.

Nevertheless, it's safe to assume that you are going to want to talk to a psychic. You and three thousand two hundred and eighty-seven other people. That's the number of callers I spoke with during my first year as a telephone psychic. Let's do a little math and get a better overview of the situation. Remember, I fielded every one of those 3,287 calls by myself. Now, consider this: The twenty-four-hour-a-day psychic network I work for—one of several dozen in our nation—has over a thousand operators fielding their calls. Multiply that by the hours in a day, the days in a week, the weeks in a year. In a recent issue of *Harper's Magazine*, it was noted that "Telecommunication analysts estimate that the psychic hot lines gross about $1 billion a year, and revenues are expected to double by the end of the century." That's a staggering amount of telephone-keypad punching. A lot of otherworldly advice. If I sit back and let my imagination run amok, I envision the fiber-optic threads that crisscross and link telephones across America, glowing and humming with an eerie blue radiance that indicates uncertainty hoping to be assuaged. And who can blame us?

Here's my take on the big existential issue of futures: When we peel back the picture or image that we have of ourselves—the one that depicts us living our safe, scheduled, and fairly routine lives—we come face-to-face with a spooky reality. We are all, individually and collectively, slowly inching toward the Great Unknown. Now, that's the core truth. And I don't care if you're Christian, Buddhist, Islamic, or a former Waco Texas groupie—no one escapes this fact. Nietzsche, in a metaphorical way, addressed this axiom that we are not the center of the universe—controlling and running our lives—when he wrote, "Since Copernicus man has been rolling from the center toward X."

We keep our feelings of uncertainty and anxiety at bay by taking care of business, organizing, designing, outlining, and purchasing those newly revised, executive-version Day-at-a-Glance planners. But did you ever hear this cute little New Age riddle?

"How do you make God laugh?"

"Tell Her your plans."

Good one, huh? But unnervingly true, wouldn't you say? One of my 3,287 callers shared that joke with me last month, right after she'd asked me how she could find solace after the sudden death of her husband.

So it's not hard to imagine why psychic networks are so ubiquitous. When a fissure appears in our seemingly seamless and well-ordered lives, we get antsy and start dialing. I usually go into this little spiel whenever some incredulous person corners me at a party and starts making fun of the popularity of electronic oracles. I know right away that they've never had their boat rocked very hard. But life rarely lets any of its children ride unscathed; sooner or later the floor caves in, the trust fund dries up, and a spouse ends up in jail. Chances are they'll be calling then, too.

3

Take This Job and . . . Love It

The first thing in life is to assume a pose.
What the second one is, no one has yet discovered.
Oscar Wilde

The secret of business is to know something that nobody else knows.
Aristotle Onassis

The résumé for my twenty-year contribution to the American work force reads like Quentin Tarantino's list of character options for his next movie. Short of "brain surgeon," I've tried my hand at just about every conceivable job available to the physically unchallenged.

I've worked in a car wash, a bakery, a Burger King *and* McDonald's, a chiropractor's office, and an automotive-supply shop. Driven a fork-lift and a moving van. Pushed my way into the big leagues to design and manage advertising for corporate lawyers and architects. Been art director for network-affiliate television stations and graphic designer for starving theater companies. Moved to New York and modeled for one of Japan's largest cosmetic firms. Edited an arts-and-leisure magazine. Worked as a professional astrologer and tarot counselor, ciphering cosmic influences for celebrities and politicians. Answered the telephone for a smarmy matchmaking service. Written travelogues and book reviews for a newspaper. Acted as a pop-music critic. Hosted a television show for kids. Published my own metaphysical journal. Sold advertising for a gay-and-lesbian monthly magazine. Became the minister of my own church. Assistant-managed two popular recording studios, one in Los Angeles, the other in Honolulu. Painted houses and abstract art. Just to name a few.

I remember one day discovering a letter that my friend Bob sent to a mutual friend. I flinched when I came across his written description of me as a "dilettante." I was angry because I felt like he was limiting my options. A shrink told me once that I had a classic *Puer Aeternus* air about me. And I countered by saying that I'd never worn that cologne before in my life. But none of my vocational dalliances came close to matching the bizarre amalgam of qualities awaiting my new position of electronic oracle.

What each of my former jobs had in common was their milieu. In any given situation I worked with customers or managers who had some common aim or function specific to the job. But on the psychic lines the sundry partitions that divide one class of people from another are obliterated. Seconds after answering I'm plunged down a rabbit hole of multidimensional human possibilities and personality types. It's what I love about the job. But at the end of a busy day, often I lie on my bed with a cool cloth against my forehead and take comfort in the uniformity of the flat, blank, stuccoed ceiling above me. I guess you could say it all depends on the caliber of calls I receive. And the numbers: too many, or too few. Both situations offered unique versions of exhilaration and stress. But the good news is: I'm never bored.

My paranormal telephone sojourn began after a friend explained how he was working for a psychic network out of Florida. His call was serendipitous—arriving three days before I moved to Seattle. I remember standing in my kitchen in Honolulu amidst a pile of half-packed boxes and trash, excitedly trying to find a pencil to jot down the name and number of his manager. The notion intrigued me. For years I'd wondered what, exactly, telephone psychics did—who they talked to and what they talked about. I also liked the idea of working out of my home and combining my metaphysical counseling skills with my inveterate love of gossip. With my free time I could read all the books in the world that I'd always wanted to read, continue to work on my journalistic enterprises, and take my time exploring my new home. I figured that I'd invest a month or two of my psychic skills until I settled into the Seattle job market. That was more than a year ago.

Friends want to know why I've remained on the phones so long. My pat response: "The money is good." And that's true. But on those days when I loathe the job, the callers, and my ball-and-chain association with the phone, I'm less gracious: "I'm bipolar, mildly masochistic, and suffer from a Tourette-like habit of speaking in tongues." And other days it's somewhere between those two responses: "I'm a curious kind of guy who enjoys hobnobbing with strangers while working as a wizard—and I'm gonna write a book about it."

The Connecting Tool

So, imagine sitting by a phone that has been converted into an otherworldly pipeline—and waiting for it to ring. And if rent is due soon, I'm *hoping* it will ring, and ring a lot. But this isn't typical of my old attitude. Before I started as a telepsych, I avidly avoided the phone; it always felt like an invasion. I'd turn off the ringer, have the machine screen the calls, or if I was feeling mean, just let it ring and ring and ring. In this era of answering machines, nothing irritates a person more than a phone that actually rings eight or ten or twelve times.

It's funny to consider that when phones were first invented people didn't avidly welcome them or their convenience. Public reactions to the very concept of a phone in the 1860s and 1870s wavered between fear of the supernatural and ridicule of the impractical. As historian John Brooks notes in his book *Telephone: The First Hundred Years*, "People were made uneasy by the very notion. Hearing voices when there was no one there was looked upon as a manifestation of either mystical communication or insanity." I experience both of these conditions every day.

To be honest, the idea of telephones fascinates me. They're like a big hunk of plastic ganglia just sitting there, daring you to dial and run up a forty-dollar bill talking to your friend on the other side of the world. Or, depending on your mood, phones can be frightening and aggressive; joy-bringing or harbinger-like. You're minding your business. Doing your things. Suddenly it rings. Out of the five billion people who occupy this planet, which one is calling *you*? Or is it just a wrong number? For a phone psychic, this sort of anticipation is quadrupled. You *never* know what to expect or what strange request you are going to hear. Is it an amiable person eager for contact or a maniac with multiple personalities ready to detail their fetal implant from a recent UFO/ET abduction?

Working as a phone psychic stimulates every conceivable emotion, both primitive and evolved, known to humankind (and some animals). There are days when I love the job and can't wait to begin conversing with the world. And then there are periods when I feel like toting a thermonuclear weapon to my desk before I begin answering the phone. I picture myself omnipotent and impatient, my finger twitching above a button that, with one delicate push, can obliterate the entire infomercial-generating network in Hollywood.

I am often uplifted by the exchange with my customers, their heartfelt "Thank you, you've helped so much"—those really make my day. But then there was the time I almost lost my job after suggesting to an obnoxious customer how an enema might be the best way to solve his dilemma.

What is certain is the element of surprise: the instantaneous connections with complete strangers; the heart-to-heart talks that leave me feeling inspired about how diverse human beings can be, how humor and tragedy can coexist within the same heartbeat; the questions, the quandaries, the indomitable spirit of inquiry that drives all of us forward. It's what makes the world go round—and my telephone ring.

My Day and How It Adds Up

Naturally, given the freedom to set my own hours, I work whenever I want to. And yes, the temptation is strong to take the day off and try to make up for the lost hours tomorrow. But I've learned to discipline myself. Two or three hours a day on the phone is manageable, but five or six can be maddening. So I pace myself. Talk, break, eat, talk, break, run errands, write, talk, break, pray, and sleep. What is consistent is the inconsistency of each stretch on the phones. Within a single hour the trajectory of my calls takes me down a pothole-riddled and winding road of human predicaments, pastimes, and rude behavior. Here's a recent page from my log book and diary:

10:10 A.M.: Started late this morning after two cups of coffee. Dialed into central computer and, once again, today's daily message from the manager was an obnoxious and whiny rant about making sure each call ". . . goes as long as it possibly can. Work those calls, people! Stretch out that hold time. Just keep 'em talking." Once again non-blabbers were threatened with termination. I feel like I'm working for the Borg.

10:15 A.M.: Judy is calling from Dallas. She's having trouble with her baby-sitter. She wants to know if the teenager has been stealing "objects" from her home. "No, I don't think so, but your horoscope does highlight your tendency to be absent-minded. Maybe you've just misplaced your stash of Snickers bars."

10:37 A.M.: Unnatural, rattled breathing into the mouthpiece with a soap opera blasting full volume in the background. I yell into the phone, "Hellllloooooo. Hellllloooo." And then, "Well, I know someone is on the line, so I guess I'll just start your reading. Hmmmm, the first thing I see coming up for you is a visit to your family physician for a respiratory checkup." Hangs up.

10:42 A.M.: Carl from Wisconsin. Friendly but timid voice. He's broke and wants to win the lottery. What are his chances? I suggest, "Work with an employment counselor and then call back when you can afford paying four dollars a minute to talk with a complete stranger who might be taking you for a ride." But he assures me that if I hang up he'll just call back and find another psychic. I see his logic and go ahead and read his cards. Not a bad spread. But first I do my standard lottery reading, the one where I tell each and every gambling aficionado that I foresee years and years of failed attempts. They usually hang up midway through the bad news, but Carl stays on and we begin a conversation about his possibilities of going part-time with a house-painting service.

10:53 A.M.: A kid, maybe twelve or thirteen, assures me that his mother has given him permission to call. He wants to know if his mom and dad will reunite, instead of divorce, after the summer. I tell him I'll lose my job because he is under eighteen and his mom will probably be pissed when she sees the phone bill. He reiterates that she gave him the OK. Before I disconnect I offer him an escape clause when his mom gets the bill: "Offer that you will never do it again and that the phone company can put a 900-number block on the phone line, and she'll appreciate your consideration."

10:47 A.M.: Donna is bummed out in Portland. She's feeling listless and wants to find a job that will bring her the satisfaction she craves as a budding artist. "Your horoscope shows some viable opportunities coming your way at the end of the year when Jupiter moves into your tenth house. I'd suggest enrolling in some noncredit college courses to help with your computer skills. Your situation looks promising." She then has me do a reading on her aunt who is sick with Parkinson's. I tell her that her aunt is having a spiritual experience.

11:09 A.M.: Hang up.

11:13 A.M.: Born-again guy. "Mr. Jones" is very troubled and "concerned" about me and is calling to welcome my soul into the arms of Our Lord and Savior.

"Are you a Christian?" he wants to know.

"Well, that's a private matter," I explain.

"There is nothing private about practicing Satan's bidding while his snares are tightening around your mind and the fire of hell is ascending up your spine."

"That's just my kundalini revving up—but thank you for sharing. Is there something I can help you with today?"

He's stymied, but after a short pause he pulls a wild non sequitur and starts telling me about a warehouse in Los Angeles that is filled to the ceiling with aborted fetuses in glass jars and "It's people like you who are responsible for the uncontrollable murder and mayhem that plagues our nation today."

I realize I'm talking to one of those abortion-clinic-firebomber types and hang up.

11:18 A.M.: Sharon in Kentucky has just taken a punch in the mouth from her boyfriend, Ronnie. Does he still love her? Should she hang in there and "make the relationship work"? I recommend professional counseling and tell her to save her money for a long stretch of therapy. But she still wants to know if the relationship will improve. Frustrated,

I decide the best thing to do is to ditch an "official" reading and lend an ear to her litany of fears. It's heart-wrenching. Finally, after she has talked for ten minutes, I tell her that I am beginning to get a vision. "Actually, Sharon, it's a long series of numbers. Yes, the numbers are coming through crystal-clear." Slowly I read off the 800 number for a national domestic-abuse center. I explain that she should call right away, that it's urgent. "Someone is there, just waiting to talk with you. It will be a life-changing conversation," I explain. Excitedly she promises she will call and then hangs up.

11:42 A.M.: Tina is placing her purebred Doberman, Mimi, in a dog show. Will the canine place high? "Well, I've never read a dog's horoscope before, but I'm game. Let's see. Yeah, transiting Venus is trine Mimi's sun on that day. It looks good."

11:51 A.M.: Margaret from New York wants two questions answered: "How can I stop smoking crack and how can I lose weight?" Despite the fact that I thought the former would facilitate the latter, I offer yet another 800 number, this one for a drug-counseling line. But she's still concerned about the dieting thing. "I'm seeing a lot of important changes coming after you make that call to the substance-abuse center. You'll be in a new bikini within two months."

"Two months?" she complains. "That's way too long."

"Well, how about a one-piece until you get up to speed," I offer stupidly, thinking a little humor might lighten things up. She *hangs* up. It's time for a break.

4
Heaven Can't Wait

The 20th Century will have to be mystical or not at all.
ANDRE MALRAUX

Heaven has become empty space for us,
a fair memory of things that were.
But our heart glows, and secret unrest
gnaws at the root of our being.
CARL JUNG

The whole point of Camp is to dethrone the serious.
SUSAN SONTAG

I came across Andre Malraux's quote in a book I like very much: *Dialogues with a Modern Mystic,* by Mark Matousek and Andrew Harvey. I recommend this book to a lot of people who are wondering what it means to be awake and spiritually vital as we enter a new millennium.

No, Mark and Andrew don't discuss telephone psychics, but they do repeatedly allude to the spirit of Jung's quote addressing our modern-day predicament: a deep spiritual malaise combined with an equally deep spiritual cluelessness, a situation that invites people to seek out and consult presumably higher life forms such as aliens, angels, and talking dolphins or lower life forms like telephone psychics.

Remember back in March 1997 when the news was riddled with the Heaven's Gate story? Those thirty-nine men and women in San Diego who, wearing brand-new tennis shoes, poisoned themselves in order to rendezvous with a mother ship that was supposedly trailing the Hale-Bopp comet? We gawked in disbelief over the tragedy, but secretly that eerie event spoke to a muddled place within each of us. In one of the cult's videotaped testimonials, a wide-eyed female explained how she'd lived for thirty years on earth—she looked fifty in the video—but had never found what she was looking for. Thus she was ready to shed her "container" and join those friendly aliens who were to fill in the empty sky that Jung was talking about.

The more I watched the news, the more I came to understand the goofy, literal-minded impulse behind the tragedy. I mean, don't we all believe that our "true self" resides in a "better" place, somewhere just out of reach? How do we find that place? How do we get back over the rainbow again?

In an allegedly Christian nation where more alien abductions are reported every year than sightings of the Virgin Mary or Jesus—and where Prozac is dispensed like Pez—I'd say plenty of us are swimming in a similar pool of spiritual discontent. We're all waiting for some sort of intervention, otherworldly or otherwise. To paraphrase Malraux, to carry on into the next century we're going to need more of the magical, spiritual, *and* mysterious in our lives. And to paraphrase Susan Sontag, a dash of absurdity—something funny and something camp—is required to loosen the too-tight grip of the sanctimonious.

Psychic networks are a perfect blend of the comical and the mystical. They are camp New Age spirituality. Their infomercials are hokey, kooky, and (sometimes) spooky. And the promotions usually involve overly earnest, subfamous celebrities who, after their testimonials, make you laugh and go, "Yeah, right! And I'm the father of Madonna's baby!" In an oblique way, psychic networks are the bedfellows of born-again Christian tithing telethons, television talk shows, and phone-sex hot lines. Talk about a marriage of the sacred and the profane! All of these "industries" demonstrate high elements of kitsch, and all of them rake in millions of dollars every year, calling to mind people like Tammy Faye Bakker. Psychic and sex lines, television huckstering and Tammy Faye are what's great about this country. Rowdy. Colorful. Going for the gusto. Unapologetically tacky. All-American.

Just a Person

"Hi. This is Frederick, and thanks for calling. How can I help you today?"

"Hello. Yes, this is Angela, and I hope you're real."

"Yep, I'm a flesh-and-blood human being."

"Well, that's OK, I guess, but I need to know if you have, like, special powers. I want someone who can really make a difference for me. And I thought you psychics could do that."

I pause. Callers like Angela are common; they don't want to be reminded that they're talking to "just a person."

So I continue, "Well, Angela, I'm not exactly a conduit of God's golden energy of atomic power, but I can consult the tarot cards for you. Or your horoscope. Divination can be a powerful tool to assist you with your questions."

Angela sounds disappointed: "Oh, well, yeah, I guess that'll do. But I was thinking about something else. Something that could really change my life."

We talk for a while longer. I ask her to give me some specific information about her problems and questions. She begins to relax. And then fifteen minutes later we are joking about some of her unfounded fears. She tells me a story about her boyfriend who is in the military and having trouble getting home for the holidays.

"It looks like everything will work out fine," I assure her. "The cards indicate that your relationship is entering a period of growth—a deeper commitment developing between the two of you. So even if he can't make it home for Christmas, the two of you are going to do well together. Keep that in mind. I see some happy times together."

"Really?" she brightens. "I'm really glad I called. I felt sort of stupid calling a psychic, but something in me just wanted to give it a try. You know, live dangerously."

"Yeah," I said. "I hear that a lot."

Americans need to be praised for their wild abandon in trying anything. Some people might consider it gullibility, but I think our intrepid curiosity is charming—to a point. As Lisa Carver, one of my favorite pop-cultural commentators, notes in *Dancing Queen*, "Americans have forgotten what's great about being American. It's not our sensitivity. It's our impatience, our changeability, our excitement, our openness, our cheer, our sexuality, our very crassness." And I agree. If people feel like touching their television for a spiritual healing or pleasuring themselves while conversing with an electronic dominatrix or calling telephone psychics, well, let them do it. It may seem goofy, but, who knows? I've lost count of the grateful customers who said how wonderful they felt after talking about their problems in a short, ten-minute magical consultation. You never can tell when someone is ready to pop into a vision of truth or new insight. So what if it happens on a phone line? Except for the financially beleaguered, most of my callers consider their time on the phone worthwhile, fun, and entertaining. And yet a shadowy element does creep into the arrangement. And its aim is to keep those callers dialing up for more.

Too Much of the Good Thing

The mere fact that advertising is an industry proves our culture's fascination with promise and illusion. And delusion. Psychic-line promotional promises are symptomatic of a crazy kind of denial that the New Age movement seems to foster. It's a classic case of psychological splitting where the dark and unsavory aspects of life are shunned with positive affirmations and visualizations. The scholar Harold Bloom in *Omens of Millennium* describes the New Age as ". . . an endlessly entertaining saturnalia of ill-defined yearnings, . . . its origins are in an old mixture of occultism and an American Harmonial faith suspended about halfway between feeling good and good feeling."

The Old versus the New

At least Old Age religion had the devil chasing after your ass and saints walking around with bad cases of stigmata. It was colorful, dramatic, and realistically mythical. I mean, maybe you don't believe in Satan, but we all can admit to having a devilish *side* to our nature. Old Age religion addressed the ambivalent and ambiguous nature of human beings.

Old Age and New Age spirituality speak to us differently. When I accepted this fact, I began to understand why so many of us want to deny our evil moments and stay happily hugged by the light. Even though it's a tilted notion, who can blame us? With Old Age religion you get hand-me-down rhetoric, supposedly delivered by God two thousand years ago, to make you feel guilty and fearful. But a New Age encounter with a real live psychic pal might reveal that you're the reincarnated spirit of W. C. Fields or Hildegaard of Bingen.

Now, I'm not saying any of this is bad—just unrealistic. Like Carl Jung, I believe people need to establish balance in their psychological lives. Yes, you should give credence to your angelic side, but don't forget to throw your animal nature a bone or two from time to time. Otherwise there'll be hell to pay. When we suppress what we sense to be negative emotions or impulses, we also shut down our ability to experience the positive and uplifting. I think human beings were designed to sense and feel everything within the kaleidoscopic realm of emotion. Jealousy, hatred, contempt, selfishness, to name just a few, are part of our picture. If we shun or move away from those qualities, we miss the opportunity to connect with the power they represent in our psyche.

The other day I asked one of my callers if he considered himself to be a vindictive person.

"No, not at all. I'm an optimist."

Jerry seemed to be sustaining his life with a steady dose of textbook New Age philosophy. Death meant reincarnation. Betrayals meant alien interventions. Illness meant an herbal deficiency of some kind.

"What does that have to do with anything?" he asked.

"Well, you haven't told me how you feel about your girlfriend cheating on you. You mentioned your past life together, but what does that have to do with right now?"

"Everything. If I hadn't abandoned her back in Atlantis, she wouldn't have run away from me now."

"But Jerry, she didn't run away. She fell in love with another guy."

"Look, I didn't call up to talk about what's happening now. I need to understand the past—why it all happened the way it did."

Realizing I was heading for a dead end, I decided to go with the proverbial flow.

"Maybe you abandoned her in Atlantis because she abandoned you centuries before in Lemuria. Do you see the cycle here?"

"I knew it! That explains everything."

"This is your opportunity to let it all go, to break the chain. Write her a letter, wish her well, and ask her to forgive the mistake you made back in Atlantis."

"Yeah, I really messed up. If only I could go back in time and make it better."

Note to Self

Someday I'm going to invade the New Age publishing arena and crank out some new motifs. Instead of books like *Embraced by the Light*, I'm going to write something titled *Seized by the Pitch-Black Midnight*. After that I'm going to tackle that *Chicken Soup for the Soul* series and compile something like *Matzo Balls for Your Inner Torment*. I'm certain that true-to-life people will welcome the appearance of these new titles on the best-seller list—well, maybe not.

5
Dear Camille Paglia

No one wants advice—only corroboration.
John Steinbeck

As much as I enjoy the convenience of working out of my home, I miss the social context of exchanging experiences, gripes, and revelations with fellow employees. A recurrent rumor within this business is the threat of someone developing a telepsych union—not an encouraging prospect for the networks, which go out of their way to keep their psychics sequestered and ignorant of competitive pay scales. So company picnics aren't an option. But I wasn't interested in policies and politics. I wanted dialogue. And with the Internet and e-mail at my disposal, I made it my mission to break the silence barrier and connect with other operators.

In my spare time I created a Web site devoted to the art of telephone divination, and within a month I was cyber-chatting with hundreds of other operators and just about every New Age specialist in the world who would share their impressions about the electronic-oracle craze. One conversation with popular tarot author Mary Greer struck me as revealing. She viewed the psychic networks as "the piece-work of the '90s." And she thought it was intriguing to find psychic networks "linked with what could be called 'folk therapy'—the unacknowledged psychological counseling that every culture has created for itself to fill the very real needs of the people."

I had to agree with Greer's spin. I'm sincere with each of my callers and share whatever psychological wisdom I can glean from the tarot or their horoscope. Ethically I had a hard time reconciling the extravagant $3.99-per-minute charge, but after a month or two I stopped worrying about the financial status of my callers. I knew that if I didn't take their call they'd just redial and connect with someone who would. The fact is, they want to talk and need to be listened to. The people who call may or may not believe in the paranormal, but what's common is their effort to find an alternative approach to solving their problems. The majority of my callers are intelligent, and if not intellectually bright, they have a brand of street savvy that is commonsensical and impressive. Most of them are educated, employed, and very inquisitive. They are also vulnerable; most wear their hearts on their sleeves. I believe that a person who is taking the time to admit quandaries and to explore options and remedies is on the right track—psychic lines or not. So let the calls begin.

Journalists always take the cheap, shockumentary approach when reporting about psychic networks. Every exposé paints the same picture: the lovesick, loopy, and lost dialing furiously to connect with some rogue waiting to snare and stall them long enough to make enough money to purchase a new Acura. Even NPR's "This American Life" stooped to the same tabloidy approach in a recent airing where an overly distressed-sounding Ira Glass interviewed a repentant telepsych about his con game. Sure, random duping happens on the phones, but there are ne'er-do-wells in every occupational field—bogus doctors, dubious contractors, sloppy homemakers, bad writers. But that's a moot point in the face of the incredibly wild popularity of the psychic networks. People need advice. And often they want it from an otherworldly source. Most of them can't afford a hundred bucks an hour every week to sort our their "issues" with a shrink. And so they call.

Dear Camille Paglia

Sociological firebrand and pop-cultural aficionado Camille Paglia agrees. I sent this letter to her "Ask Camille" column on *Salon* magazine's Web site:

> *I recently started work as a telephone oracle for one of those ubiquitous psychic networks you see advertised every evening in the late-night-television slush zone. I can't help but wonder what techno-prophet Marshall McLuhan would have thought about this form of electronic divination. In lieu of Mr. McLuhan, I figured you'd be the next best authority to approach with my question. So what gives? What does the wild popularity of this new American pastime represent?*

Her response was nearly immediate, and it corroborated my philosophy about psychic phone psychology. She wrote:

> *...Your professional precursors sat at Delphi and Cumae and were god-blessed wonders of the ancient world. . . . As a '60s zealot of the mystic sciences (astrology, palmistry,* I Ching, *tarot, et al.), I'm delighted with the boom in psychic divination. . . . Telephone psychics function as populist psychiatrists for the lower-middle and working classes, who can't afford either the time or the money required for the kind of systematic, superindulgent therapy that has become such a cliché of middle-class life in the United States. . . ."*

Paglia also pointed out that most believers in psychic assistance feel the spiritual, emotional, and intellectual insufficiencies of both traditional and organized religion. Yep, as I've said before, we want something both profound *and* entertaining. And instantaneous.

6
The Body Electric

The universe is made up of stories, not atoms.
MURIEL RUCKEYSER

My friends complain that watching television with me is like sitting in front of a giant strobe light. Like most Americans, I'll usually stop my hair-triggery channel surfing for one of three on-screen happenings: nearly naked people, nearly naked and/or clothed people who are caught in a car chase or an explosion, and a psychic-network infomercial. The last has a strange effect on me: it's an anachronistic twang—an archetypal pull toward fringe subjects like oracles, gypsies, fortune-telling, and the old Psychic Friends Network's Linda Georgian's hair size.

My fascination is doubly embarrassing because (1) I'm already a mystic well aquainted with the possibilities and limitations of stuff like astrology and the tarot, and (2) I'm aware of how the cheesy advertisements are designed to capitalize on our fears and hopes, and yet, once on my screen, I can't turn the spellbinding commercials off. I think this is why I transformed so easily from insomniac infomercial-watching couch potato to magical, vibrant, telephone-psychic-maven chair potato. Despite the corny hokum of the infomercials, I knew that the potential was there for something genuine to take place between the caller and the psychic—should the psychic be any good. So, I thought, I might as well be that psychic.

It's funny how people who embrace horoscopes, the *I Ching*, angel cards, and dowsing for water with unraveled wire hangers will stop and ask me how delivering a reading over the telephone could be effective. My answer is that they're being too literal-minded. They think time and space apply in the otherworld, as if someone calling from Dallas is too distanced from me in Seattle to receive a genuine reading. And so they quiz me: "Don't you have to be in the same room with the person? Don't you need more of a connection than just the sound of a voice?"

Personally, I don't have any trouble with the viability of a telephone as a divination tool. I consider the world, the universe, everyone and everything in it, as one big writhing mass of synchronous interconnection. Traditionally, someone who relates to reality like this is considered "enlightened," but I'm not saying that this is necessarily the case with me. Still, I can grock the concept of an all-pervasive unity with ease, and this is what I try to explain to people who press me for a reason—that distance doesn't matter, because everything and everyone is linked. So, whether in the same room, across town, or from the bottom of the ocean, readings can and will be delivered—I've got a car payment to make.

As a pre-millennial, sociologically minded astrologer watching Uranus and Neptune move through the sign Aquarius, I know that a global renaissance is underway. A new way of thinking and feeling about ourselves is spreading through the buzz and circuitry of our love affair with all things electronic. This renaissance is not taking place within science, politics, art, or a new world order, although these fields might be affected by its evolution. I'm talking about a spiritual movement, a jolt to our collective nervous system that is unequivocally mystical. It's nonsecular renewal intertwining with our burgeoning Information Age. As Canadian techno-sociologist Marshall McLuhan said in *The Medium Is the Message,* "All media are extensions of some human faculty—psychic or physical." Through simple correlation McLuhan explained that "The wheel is an extension of the foot, the book is an extension of the eye . . . clothing, an extension of the skin . . . electric circuitry, an extension of the nervous system."

And I agree. Computers, pocket beepers, cell phones, fax machines, and psychic networks are symbols of our evolving neuro capacities. Nerves are what make humans human; the bigger the ball of nerves at the base of the neck (i.e., the brain), the less—for most of us—bestial we appear, think, and feel.

According to quantum physicists, humans are nothing more than vibrating bits of electrical impulses with "voices" that sound back and forth and make synapses. And biologists tell us that when one person's body touches another person's body, chemicals under the skin break down and recombine, setting off an electric spark that jumps, neuron to neuron, to the brain. Is that really any different from what happens when your finger pushes the buttons on a keypad that sends signals across a telephone wire to my apartment in Seattle? So when I hit a button on *my* keyboard, we are very much touching one another. Think about this the next time someone tells you that they've gotten out of the shower to answer your call.

7

A Little History, A Little Sex

We have not lost our ancient need to see behind the curtain.
All that has changed is that we now have industries that lift it for us,
or at least for some of us, every day, for a price.

JAMES B. TWITCHELL

Here's my phantasmagoric vision of the cosmological events that precipitated the birth of a psychic-loving nation: The moon moved into the seventh house. Jupiter aligned with Mars. Peace was guiding the planets, and love was goading the stars. The earth trembled and glowed, while Neptune and Uranus entwined and shimmied. And hovering above these epic, intergalactic happenings was a giant fetus—remember the movie *2001*?—enclosed in a transparent, egglike sphere.

Did this happen in Las Vegas during a neonatal nursing convention? Nope, this was the birth of the Age of Aquarius—and of Dionne Warwick's foray into the world of late-night infomercials. The year? 1991.

OK, so I'm exaggerating a bit, but I don't think it's such a big coincidence for a new astrological age to begin just as a psychic network is born. As a planetary watcher, it's my job to scan the heavens and try to make sense of the startling events that make living on this planet so intriguing. And I remember thinking to myself, when I saw the first

Psychic Friends Network infomercial, "*Finally*, here's more evidence of the highly touted Age of Aquarius."

Technically speaking, an astrological age begins or ends whenever the point of the vernal equinox progresses into a new constellation of the zodiac. (Just stay with me on this!) Astronomers explain the phenomenon as a subtle shift in our collective perspective of the universe. But astrologers get all excited because that shift means we're collectively moving from one age to another. So what? Well, symbolically a new age represents a tremendous turning point within the spiritual ethos of our global community. Look at the cultural changes that followed the European Renaissance and you'll have a small-scale idea of why the Aquarian age has generated so much excitement.

Because each age spans approximately a 2,150-year period, the actual threshold between ages is difficult to pinpoint. And because the last Aquarian age happened, oh, 25,000 years ago, no one is around to tell us what *that* cosmic shindig was like. So astrologers can only speculate on the apparent effects of the current transition. We take notes, swap data, and do what all prophets do: watch for signs. I feel that the initial portents of the Aquarian age coincided with the discovery of electricity and the launch of the Industrial Revolution. Those were profound cultural and scientific transformations that set the stage for yet another phase in humankind's evolution. They were also events that have everything to do with the intrinsic qualities of the sign Aquarius.

What's in an Age

Each sign of the zodiac has a cluster of myths that mirror its essential core. Astrologers access these myths when they talk astrology. The Greek myth of Prometheus corresponds most strongly to the sign Aquarius. Prometheus was memorable because he stole fire from the gods and shared it with human beings on earth so they could improve their lot in life. In modern times that gift of fire corresponds to the power and mystery of electricity. And in our era, electricity has literally brightened and uplifted the way we live—for all the reasons you already know. Pick your favorite: light bulbs, electric knives, televisions, microwave ovens, computers, and so on and so forth. My favorite? The telephone, of course.

During the fading Piscean age, which commenced around the birth of Jesus, religion and devotion were humankind's main vehicles to establish a connection with God. But with the new Aquarian age, knowledge has taken the place of faith. Technology, with the ability of the computer and telephone to decentralize and interconnect, will play a central role in adjusting our spiritual perception of the world around us. I know it seems far-fetched, but remember that we are living in a transitional phase between the two ages. It might be hard to see clearly what the new aeon portends, but clues can be found in the musings of our poets, artists, and prophets—individuals who are already feeling the shock of the new.

How Dionne Circumvented San Jose and Really Hit the Big Time

Every culture has a unique oracular medium. The Chinese forged intricate coins. The Italians created cryptically illustrated tarot cards. The Greeks consulted an oracle at Delphi. Nordic cultures picked engraved runes from a pouch. Americans? We have our impatience, a phone, and Dionne Warwick.

And I just *had* to talk to her.

When I heard that Dionne was in Seattle searching for a new home, I bugged Linda, a realtor friend, to help me track her down.

"There's so much I want to ask her," I told Linda.

"Well, if you meet her, bring a gas mask, because my associate who is showing her properties says she smokes like a chimney."

I ignored that cheap shot. "I really want to know how she became interested in metaphysics. Maybe I could even look at her horoscope. I wonder how she feels about being the queen mother of the psychic networks?"

I never did meet Dionne, and she never did move to Seattle. Her Psychic Friends Network filed for bankruptcy and she went to another part of America—South America. But I still kept at it. I eventually called her manager, Marie, in Los Angeles and asked if she could set up an interview.

"Whatever for?" She sounded genuinely perplexed.

"Well, I'm writing a book, and I'm including a section on the history of the psychic lines. So I want to know why Ms. Warwick decided to become involved—what her spiritual impetus was."

"Oh, well, I can answer that for you. The company that owns the lines offered her a tremendous amount of money."

I was disheartened but not surprised. As Bertolt Brecht said, "Grub first, then ethics."

If there were a temple of the electronic oracle, Dionne Warwick would be the high priestess. I think kudos are in order for her intrepid spirit. Warwick brought prestige and viability to a field that, at the time, was a completely unproven commodity. Inphomation, the company that hatched one of the first psychic networks back in 1991, was onto something tremendous when they married our culture's wild interest in the New Age with available technology. With a tiny pool of approximately thirty psychics, the company started running short commercials on cable television. Three years later, Inphomation's annual sales figures topped $100 million. It's purported that Warwick has made more money from her psychic-network gig than all the rest of the money combined from her impressive pop-music career.

Talk Dirty to Me

But before there were gigantic, glamorous, celebrity-fueled psychic networks, there were modest, down-home psychic "hot lines" staffed with a small number of operators. And before there were phone psychics there was . . . *ta-da* . . . phone sex.

I've interviewed network executives, veteran operators, and promotional directors, but no one seems to know when the first psychic line set up shop. Yet my friend Sheila, who manages a network out of Florida, told me that the outrageous success of the dial-a-porn industry in the late '80s gave rise to the initial gaggle of psychic operators.

"The first psychic hot line was based in San Diego and started around 1990," she explained. "It was a boiler-room situation, and this was before the technology was in place that allowed the psychics to work out of their homes. I know that one of the companies had sex operators on one floor and psychics on another."

So, not surprisingly, it was a Californian who had the brilliant idea of replacing the (imagined) pre-coital, big-breasted blonde who fielded the phone-sex calls with an imaginative, caring, and genuine psychic pal who could also deal attentively with the callers' other wild desires—their dreams about money and career and their odds for dating someone with the equivalent sex appeal of that big-breasted blonde.

When you think about it, this historical correlation makes perfect sense. The writer Patricia Meyer Spacks once said, "Gossip, even when it avoids the sexual, bears around it a faint flavor of the erotic." And my friend Vedika agrees: "The psychic lines are sort of sensual," she notes. "You're talking to a stranger. It's personal. It's intimate. Their voice is right there in your ear. The link between the two situations isn't that disparate. One's a genital link, the other telepathic. They both involve merging with a stranger."

And that's how it works: It's late at night. You're home alone. You see the infomercial on television, and you want some attention. Who are you going to call?

Info Junkies

People also want contact with information—tons of it. The entire pay-per-call 900 industry was designed to meet our culture's wild hunger for timely, easily accessed info-bites. The idea that we are acquiring something—be it gossip or facts—appeals to our old Piscean-age hunting-and-gathering instincts, which slowly are being replaced with the Aquarian ideal that knowledge is more valuable than things. See how that whole age-transition thing works?

And what kind of info-bites? Secrets of sex and the soul, of course. Statistics show that the pay-per-call industry's sex and psychic divisions are consistently ranked the most profitable and stalwart. Joke, racing, and health-tip lines may wax and wane, but the libidinal and the otherworldly never lose their allure—racking up billions of dollars each year.

According to industry expert Robert Mastin in his book *900 Know-How*, the public's first blanket exposure to the 900 prefix was during the Reagan-Carter presidential debates in 1980. Callers from the television-viewing audience phoned in their "vote" for each candidate and paid fifty cents for the privilege. Five hundred thousand calls flooded the computer switchboard. And AT&T, receiving a cut on each call, was very happy. Gigantic dollar signs flashed. Those three little digits really paid off.

Seven years later, AT&T made out like a cyber-bandit when they devised an elaborate accounting system known as premium billing service. This arrangement allowed a 900 business to leave all of their accounting worries and collection procedures firmly in AT&T's hands. Suddenly the telecommunications giant had become a default credit-card provider. People called. The psychic networks provided. And like an electronic godfather, AT&T billed, collected, and dispersed the money, keeping a good percentage of every dollar.

Two months into my phone-wizard career, I began entertaining the idea of opening my own psychic line. Over the years I'd become well-versed in advertising and design. And certainly I knew how to give a psychic reading. So why not get in on some of that big money? I'd start my own line, do all the promotion, hire the operators, and then—go bankrupt.

If you talk to anyone who runs a 900 business, you'll most likely hear a protracted story of high hopes dashed on the rocks of hidden costs and poor planning. And it's true: reality checks are in order. The most damaging liability within the fiber-optic-oracle biz is the "charge-back" condition that plagues any information provider utilizing a service bureau and billing arrangements with one of the mainstream phone utilities.

OK, a little explanation of jargon is required here: *Information provider* is a telecommunications term used to define any business that offers information or entertainment to a caller. A *service bureau* is like a miniature phone company. They own all the equipment and computers that handle the calls for the various companies who use their routing services. And "various" is putting it mildly. Service bureaus don't discriminate. Their client roster includes Prayer of the Day right alongside Monica's Telephone Sex Tips and Favorite Bathroom Humor's Joke of the Day. And, of course, your favorite psychic line.

When a customer dials the 900 number, the call is first routed through the psychic network's service bureau. Then it is transferred to the phone carrier, who delivers the call to one of the various psychics working at their apartment, home, or padded cell. Each of these links and transfers involves a fee, comprising nearly a dollar of the standard $3.99-per-minute rate.

No Need to Pay

Real problems for the psychic lines began in 1993 after the Federal Communications Commission tightened up its consumer-protection provisions. Besides defining illegal practices, the new standards prohibited disconnection of phone services for nonpayment of 900-line charges. In the biz this new provision became known as the "charge-back." And here's an example of how it works:

I once took a late-night call from a crazy guy in New York who somehow had managed to sneak his local pool hall's cordless telephone into the men's bathroom. Hidden behind a stall, he proceeded to yack with me for an hour about his dream to co-star with Tom Cruise in a sci-fi film that he was "going to sell to the highest bidder." No one was the wiser, well, until the owners of the bar received their phone bill a month later. Did they have to pay for that psychic-line psychobabble-fest? Nope. They probably just disputed the charge. And this meant the psychic network not only lost their hundred-dollar fee but still had to pay me *and* the service bureau *and* their phone-service provider for conducting and carrying the call.

Savvied and sneaky psychic-line customers have turned the charge-back situation into a fun-filled hobby. They call the psychic lines, blabbing until the sun comes up, and then they blame their ten-year-old for unwittingly placing the call after becoming "confused" watching an infomercial. And the phone company usually drops the fee off of the phone bill—and then turns around and forwards the charge to the psychic network. Many outraged telecommunications managers consider this charge-back regulation a license to steal granted by the federal government. Consumer-affairs people consider it symptomatic of the deceptive advertising gimmicks employed by the networks. Regardless, charge-backs account for millions of dollars in lost revenue for the psychic networks—another reason for their steep per-minute fee.

The Grand Total

Now, tabulate the costs of advertising, insurance, legal fees, rent, copy machines, office supplies, and computers. Then figure the salaries and fees of executives, secretaries, managers, bookkeepers, psychics, janitors, and Valium prescriptions, and it's easy to see how those imagined monster profits begin to dwindle into puny little margins.

And yet, plenty of profit remains. Do the psychics receive their fair share of the big money? This is a debate that rages on and on in the business. My answer: It depends on the company that's running the line. Like sweatshop slaves, the psychic's pay depends on the industry's current bottom line. Decent compensation for an operator in the '90s was around thirty to forty cents per minute of talk time. That's a nice eighteen to twenty-four bucks an hour. But I've watched that rate drop steadily throughout the latter part of the '90s. As Camille Paglia noted in her *Salon* column, "It's pretty clear that the field is in Gold Rush chaos, with charlatanry liberally mixed with the genuine article." And this trickery has little to do with the psychics who field the calls—although there are plenty of dubious operators out there. The false claims, bait-and-switch tactics, and blatant lying that engage or enrage the public are symptomatic of the growing competition in the field. Where there were very few psychic lines back in the early '90s, there are probably several hundred today.

Paranormal-fueled business ventures aren't suited to the ethics of capitalism. Graft, con, and misleading advertising are conditions that plague the electronic-oracle racket. During my stint on the lines, I've experienced slipshod management and pressure for performance that could be considered threatening. And I've left networks because of their manipulative direct-mail campaigns that scare gullible customers into calling by preying on their fear of the supernatural. I've also been ripped off when an employer closed shop and disconnected the phones, leaving me in the lurch for pay that was owed to me. As vocations go, I sometimes think that I myself need a psychic to maneuver the choppy, murky waters that churn the oceans of the oracular networks.

There's an indestructible spirit to the psychic lines, fostered by our culture's archetypal fascination with their "product." It's an intrigue that continues to grow, mutate, and spread. Run a search on the World Wide Web and you'll discover thousands of cyber-psychics offering everything from garden-variety telephone readings to astral-body hex removals, voodoo love charms, and psychospiritual therapy e-mail sessions. Several of the nation's larger networks have moved to the Internet as well, setting up high-tech Web sites that despite their electronic interface still resemble an overstocked Santería shop. Not surprisingly, America Online recently opened its first pay-per-link psychic-reading forum to accommodate thousands of curious customers hankering for a chat exchange with a psychic. And shortly before her death, Jeanne Dixon, America's favorite soothsayer, leased her name to an online company designed to provide the curious with live, one-on-one, "videoconferenced" metaphysical counseling sessions.

It's funny to consider that in only a decade telephone psychics have become a normal fixture within the landscape of American businesses which offer needed services to a constant stream of regular customers. Like dentists, optometrists, psychiatrists, short-order cooks, and carnival Ferris-wheel operators, telephone psychics are here to stay. The big oracle networks have become a permanent fixture within our culture's burgeoning love affair with all things New Age circuited through the techno-age *zeitgeist*.

8

I Was a Teenage Pagan

Do not think that there is more in destiny than
can be packed into a childhood.
RAINER MARIA RILKE

Pictures sometimes reveal *too* much. Years ago I was visiting my mom in California and spent a Sunday afternoon with her exploring boxes of old family photographs. Amidst the reminiscing and laughs I froze in shock when I came across an old black-and-white picture taken of me when I was maybe three or four years old. There I was, without a shirt, in my grandmother's living room, standing on the arm of a couch, hugging a Bible to my chest with one hand and raising my other hand in a sort of Eva Perón salute. I was also wearing a petticoat.

Presumably, according to my mother, I was imitating the priest from our church.

"A priest in a petticoat?"

"Oh, that was just your version of his fancy robes. Weren't you cute?" she said. "You haven't changed a bit, you know."

"I haven't changed a bit?"

"Well, no. I've never known what to expect from you."

People are curious about what would drive a person to become a telephone psychic. And believe me, the question echoes through my head all the time. Maybe that photo holds the symbolic key: an intoxication with religiosity, a flare for the dramatic, an identification with the feminine—and a lust for power. It's easy to see the psychological wiring that led me to the phones. All the components were already in place.

First of all, I was an only child until I was eight years old. It's common that people with pronounced psychic abilities were left alone or felt lonely as children. This solitude engendered, in my case, a rich fantasy life where I turned inward for company. In learning to talk to myself, in my imagination, I learned how to talk to others.

Second, I was an oddball. I hated school, was a mediocre student, and was tormented by other children who accused me of looking like an alien because my eyes were tiny and deep-set. I also had a penchant for showy attire, arriving at school dressed like a miniature version of Quentin Crisp—which only added to my disenfranchised state.

To complicate matters, I had an eccentric interest in all things occult and mystical. While other boys were hoarding baseball cards, I was collecting those tiny annual Dell sun-sign guides, popular with housewives and the lovelorn. In lieu of typical childhood aspirations, I was contemplating how I could summon nature spirits or discarnate entities to assist in my quest to penetrate the secrets of the universe.

But fundamentally, the driving force behind my fascination with mysticism was an early and abiding attraction to and identification with the feminine realm. Naturally, this made it very hard to be a boy in a man's world.

From the age of five to thirteen, I was raised by my divorced mother and grandmother, two women who practiced an unconscious and subtle suburban witchcraft. I remember late-afternoon sessions with the Ouija board, hugging trees in the backyard at moments of family crisis, and the potent gossip that is the modern equivalent of hexes and spell casting. So reaching into the intuitive side of my nature in order to relate was perfectly acceptable behavior.

The dawning of the Age of Aquarius coincided with my own coming of age. Sybil Leek, a witch, and Sydney Omar, an astrologer, became my idols as a teenager. Leek's *My Life in Astrology* was a vibrant testament that a living could be forged within a fringe field. And Omar's trenchant ability to write about astrology as if it were an empirical science left a strong impression on me.

Once, when I heard that Omar was to be the featured guest on a popular talk-radio show, I stayed up all night dialing until finally I was put through to the studio. I wanted to ask him some questions. It was my first foray into using the telephone as a probe. He supported my interest in astrology but added that I should be diligent with my schoolwork because "You're going to need a day job." I recorded the conversation on cassette and played it over and over.

By age thirteen, I was a full-blown mama's boy. And people were concerned. I guess that the infamous petticoat photo must have made the rounds of family members. Finally, reenacting one of those ancient tribal rituals, I was dragged away from the maternal nest and forced to live with my father. I was uncomfortable with this new arrangement. Within a day I'd been jettisoned from my mother's mystical, gauzy world and into my father's Spartan, analytical one. To compensate for my shock, I was given my own room at the top of my father's house. How did I see myself? As Rapunzel trapped in an ivory tower.

Where my mother was intuitive and spontaneous, my father was scientific and tough, the kind of guy who could be chewing a mouthful of bologna sandwich and still dislodge plaster off the walls with the power of his voice. He was constantly yelling up the stairwell to my room, "Jesus Christ! What in God's name are you doing up there!" I wasn't doing my homework. I was playing with tarot cards or scratching my head over my newly arrived astrology correspondence course.

To my father's credit, he did make efforts to support my eccentric interests. As a bonding gesture, he would make dutiful pilgrimages to head shops and hippie boutiques for my birthday. Imagine this former Notre Dame linebacker combing the shelves for tarot decks, black-light posters of the galaxy, and spinning mobiles with an astrological motif. A good sport!

All the while, however, he was trying to steer my inquiring mind away from mysticism and toward philosophy—namely, the German philosophers Immanuel Kant and my namesake, Friedrich Nietzsche.

Somehow the tomes of these intellectual giants didn't mesh well with my dog-eared copy of *Linda Goodman's Sun Signs*. Kant was beyond my reach, but there were qualities to Nietzsche's militant cosmologies that fed my nascent sense of human destiny.

California Dreamin'

At sixteen, during my first camping trip with a group of friends, my destiny unfurled before me like a yellow brick road. I awakened to the realization that my father's aspirations for my future had nothing to do with mine. Every parent, deep down, wants his or her child to fulfill the parent's own unfulfilled dreams. My father was no exception. Despite his successful career as an engineer, he longed to be a doctor. He devoted many long hours in our garage working on medical inventions, ingenious contraptions that never saw the light of day because, in the end, he considered humanity undeserving. So he saw me heading for medical school. But I knew I was irrevocably off to see the wizard.

After returning from my rocky-mountain-high, I packed my bags and announced to my father that I was moving in with my friend Bernice, a middle-aged, vodka-loving fellow occultist, and her family. I spent the summer after my graduation in their beached Winnebago on the front lawn. As I look back I wonder: Was this a foreshadowing of my future vocation as oracle for America's trailer-park culture?

Soon, through Bernice's efforts, I was deeply entrenched in the Southern California metaphysical community. I was hobnobbing and tossing back highballs with instructors and authors and was editing a monthly astrological newsletter. Gradually I became part of the paranormal-lecture circuit, delivering precocious talks on sociological planetary influences and offering advice on how astrology might be taught to younger people. I suppose I was considered a prodigy, but I felt more like the Tom Thumb of the psychic underground.

Bernice and I would drive once a week to Hollywood, where our astrology teacher held court in a room above her garage. The mix of students was a peculiar group of eccentrics—many of whom I can imagine working the psychic lines today. The men were in caftans or black turtlenecks and sported huge gold medallions. The women were in saris and muumuus or psychedelic shifts and capris with dangling charms and trinkets. It was a Hollywood jamboree of show-biz-wannabes, crazed spiritualists, and front-runners of the coming New Age.

Paradise Unlimited

In my twenties, I swam straight into the heart of the feminine. I moved to Hawaii, geographically the most isolated landmass on the planet and a natural oasis for outsiders. And there my spirituality thrived. Hawaii meant I was four thousand miles away from the mainland, physically and culturally secluded in a monastery of palm trees and cannabis sativa.

Aside from its lush climate and physical beauty, Hawaii is remarkable for the way spirituality is integrated into everyday life—in a tangible way. A building doesn't go up in Hawaii without a kahuna blessing it. Mishaps on a construction site might be attributed to the disruption of an ancient burial ground—and then discussed on the evening news. And when you hike through the glorious mountains and valleys, it's customary to leave an offering to the nature spirits who protect the terrain. Christianity, Buddhism, Polynesian traditions, and New Age teachings interweave to create a common feeling of connection to the supernatural. And like ancient Greece, the gods and goddesses of Hawaii partake in daily activities. When the volcanoes rumble, Pele, the goddess of fire, is angry.

My reputation as a dilettante blossomed in Honolulu. I studied graphic design, abstract art, secured a position with a local newspaper, opened—and closed—my own church, worked with a local theater company, and hosted a daytime television show for kids. My mystical leanings continued to burgeon. I remained a student of astrology and the tarot, and I began teaching it as well. I became deeply involved with a wide array of philosophies: Rosicrucianism, the Hawaiian healing art of Huna, Jungian depth psychology, a smorgasbord of self-improvement seminars, Zen meditation, and the teachings of G. I. Gurdjieff. This winding trajectory eventually led to my interest in the teachings of A. H. Almaas's Diamond Work—a powerful synthesis of Western and Eastern approaches to psychological and spiritual development.

Hawaii's dreamy atmosphere and lack of seasons makes one feel suspended in time. Twenty years passed, and I knew it was time to return to the mainland. I imagined myself sipping coffee with like-minded, forward-moving artists, conferring with computer aficionados, and furthering my career as a writer. But as usual, one's fantasies don't always mesh with reality. I needed a job. My savings were dwindling and I felt unmotivated to re-create myself as the person I'd been. So fate reshuffled the cards, dialed my number, and, well, you know the rest of the story.

And so here I sit in my sweatpants, smoking a cigarette. The phone is definitely unplugged today. It's a cloudy Seattle afternoon, and Madonna's latest CD is on the stereo. I'm waiting for my current group of oddball friends to arrive for dinner. And tonight, invariably, we'll discuss the meaning of life. Not much has changed.

I guess you could say I'm a little more integrated now. It's a harmony that has been difficult to achieve. Perhaps my lengthy sojourn in Hawaii and all those years of meditation, study, and therapy have contributed to my status as a fairly sane—albeit true-blue—middle-aged pagan.

9
Tonight, Make It Lowbrow

What fresh hell is this?
DOROTHY PARKER

A novice phone psychic is considered the low person on the network's telephone pole. And that's not a pretty place to reside. I'll explain.

One of the biggest myths—one that I believed too, at first—about this job is the promise of easy money. In the beginning, I thought I'd hire on with a network, purchase a headset, pop out my tarot cards, and recline while the phones rang and the checks came rolling in. But it doesn't work that way. Dues must be paid. And this means working the middle-of-the-night graveyard shift, which means talking to every sloppy drunk, truculent insomniac, spittle-spewing zealot—and the occasional normal person—who happens to be up at four in the morning, bored out of their gourd, and ready for psychic intervention. Although occasionally charming, sometimes startling—but usually pity-evoking—my graveyard coterie became a true test of my angelic compassion—and devilish retaliation.

As in any other job, scratching and clawing your way up to the top is a given. And a phone psychic is continually forced to toggle between ethics and a big paycheck. I found this predicament to be the most unsavory requirement in the business. Network managers use a system of averages to determine who will receive calls and who won't—or, to put it another way, who will make money and who won't. And this is another part of the dues-paying policy.

Finding a Niche

In the beginning, all new psychics must prove their "worth" to the company. This means that the operators who yack the longest will receive a consistent flow of calls. Those with long hold times, which means keeping people on the line for an average of thirty minutes or more, will be put in the company's high-priority "hot zone." Psychics with low averages are thrown into the slush pool, or as one company called it, "purgatory," where only the most desperate, cretin psychics will stay logged on waiting for a call to find them. If they're lucky they might receive a call or two, and God help these callers as the psychics apply all of their wiles to stretch the length of the calls.

So, if there are four thousand psychics working for a company, and you've just started, you can bet you're going to have a priority number around 3,999. And this means that the 3,998 operators above you are going to get a crack at a customer before the other calls drip down to your pitiful little pool.

Since no one wants to work graveyard, you'll find a smaller number of operators working after midnight. This means that as a newcomer you have a greater chance of receiving calls and building up your hold time during the wee hours. But who wants to be up at three in the morning listening to a blurry-brained stranger—who just peaked on her third Percodan—ramble on about her fourth marriage to a Russian immigrant who never takes her out dancing and hates her pet poodle Kootchie? Nobody who doesn't have to.

The lower ranks of the network are filled by newbies, and if you work long enough in this business there are lots of newbie moments. Why? Because psychic networks can be like gypsies, folding up shop and moving to another state where the tax laws are more lenient. Or going bankrupt and then, a month later, resurfacing with a new name and the same old data bank of customers. The worst just disappear completely, screwing the psychics out of their pay, never to be heard from again. I've witnessed all of these metamorphoses during my year on the phones.

"Please Hold"

Of course, you can imagine that all of this rallying for priority and call volume generates strange behavior from the destitute psychics who need to feed their children and pay off their cars. My favorite story involves an industrious female operator who would answer the phone and inform the caller that all of the psychics were busy and "please hold on." She'd assure the customer that they wouldn't be charged, mute her phone, and then go back to watching Susan Powter's latest infomercial. Not knowing any better, the caller would dangle for about five minutes. Then she'd get back on the line, light some incense, diddle some wind chimes, and prepare for a "short meditation period" that was supposed to really get her mojo running. The meditation would go on for another five minutes. Already she'd bagged about four dollars on the call and the customer had spent forty. Finally, she'd be raring to go. I can't imagine the sort of reading she gave, but a caller naïve enough to hang on the line could have been told anything. I heard this story from the very customer it happened to. And yes, I've got to say, he wasn't a brain donor.

Bad Behavior

Say you are having a really bad day—or, in my case, night. You get up in the morning and feel like scum—you hate the world and the Creator that created it. And yet you still have to go to your job. Decorum and financial security dictate that—despite your crappy mood—you must be on your best behavior. Your co-workers or customers still have to interact with you, and your boss could come in any minute and catch you throwing attitude. He doesn't want to deal with your PMS, hangover, or bad temper. So you keep a lid on it. Well, in the world of psychic lines you don't have to worry about stuff like that. If you're feeling bad, you can always take it out on the customers.

Of course, this is done only with jerks—the obnoxious, belligerent, screechy callers who make the graveyard shift such a downer. So when they called, I was ready—coupling my magic and anonymity to cut loose with some startling pronouncements. Over time I noticed different classifications of post-midnight callers. When the phone was silent I'd sit at the table, pencil in hand, and list the various characteristics and quirks of each group. Eventually I narrowed it down to three main categories: Aladdin Addicts, Gimme-Gimmes, and My-Name-Is-Legions.

The Aladdin Addicts are by far the biggest group of the midnight coterie. These callers are deluded with childlike, genie-in-a-bottle expectations. They're sweet but sad, and I had to learn to be gentle with their quivering hopes and half-baked schemes. The typical Aladdin Addict is an insomniac who's watched too many psychic-line jamborees on television. They'll toss and turn and then jump out of bed to launch a fervent hunt for an operator who will support their fantasy of being inches away from meeting their soul mate, finding a bag of money in the street, or winning the Miss America pageant. Of course, finding such an operator is a pretty sure thing during the midnight shift.

The Gimme-Gimmes are typified by the money-to-burn narcissist with the personality quotient of a cigar-store Indian. They'll call, give their birthdate, and then sit stone-silent on the other end. And that's it—for nearly an hour. I'll talk and talk and try to engage them in conversation, but their only response is "Just keep going." They imagine that the psychics are locked up in a boiler room with a whip-wielding manager standing guard and barking orders like "Channel the light! Give every ounce of thy soul to thy customer!" Although great for the bucks, the Gimme-Gimmes were hell on my larynx.

The My-Name-Is-Legions are the most difficult class of customers. They include the inebriated and drug-addled right alongside the vulgar and mean-spirited. What this group has in common is a conviction that—because they're paying for it—the psychic exists solely as a recipient for their loopy or abusive behavior. If they couldn't find someone in their household to drool on or fight with at three in the morning, they'd end up calling me. Of course, I always knew where to draw the line. Or press the envelope. Or offer a cliché or two.

What Are His Chances of Landing the Woman of His Dreams?

One night in April I was working really late, trying to build up my priority with yet another new company. I bought my partner earplugs because he'd gotten tired of hearing me say things like "the Ace of Cups is covered by the Hanged Man and crossed by the Fool, and this means you shouldn't spend your money playing the lottery" all night long. And this was one of those long, long nights.

I was in an edgy mood. It was my sixth month on the job, and I was irritated with my future options and perplexed about what my situation could possibly "mean." I should have done a reading for myself, right on the spot, but then who would have paid me for that? The calls were sporadic—one every ten minutes or so: lots of hangups, shrieking teenagers, and the intermittent nice person who was "just curious" and calling to see if I was "real." I'd smoked a lot of cigarettes and thrown back a couple of beers while eating some cold pizza when another fifteen minutes went past without a call. Just when I was ready to unplug my headset, the phone rang. I answered, and before I could even finish my opening spiel the guy on the other end was snapping at me in a loud, pugnacious tone, "Come on, let's do it! I don't have all night here!"

When I explained that I needed to shuffle my cards so I could link up to his credibility field, he started to challenge my veracity—a bad move that really set me on edge.

"You know what, sir? I don't work with skeptics. I'm going to suggest that you call back and connect with another psychic."

"Why? Can't you handle a little pressure? Where's the loving light and compassionate concern I was promised?"

"Oh, I can handle pressure," I assured him. "But I'm not in the mood for being rushed right now. And as for the loving light, well, I think you've got the wrong psychic."

"Hey buddy, I'm not paying three-ninety-nine a minute for a god-damned mood. This is supposed to be about me, my future. So let's do it! I've got three minutes free here and I wanna know what you see coming up for me and this chick I just picked up downtown."

I was silent.

He continued: "So, Mr. Psychic, here's what I wanna know. Is this gal gonna go all the way with me tonight—or am I gonna end up as horny as I started?"

I made a face like I'd bitten into something foul. Pitying the "downtown chick," I leaned back in my chair and stalled while an evil impulse welled in my heart—not truly satanic exorcist-quality evil, just something mildly devious and Beelzebubian. I could feel a tiny smile starting to spread from the corners of my mouth. I began to shuffle the deck and then slowly, very slowly—excruciatingly slowly—place each card out in front of me.

I was eyeballing my digital stopwatch, waiting for it to hit the three-minute mark, and all the while I was breathing into the receiver and making barely audible sounds. "Mmmm-hmmm. The High Priestess is here, denying the resurrection of the Emperor. Oh, yes. Hmmm. I see. Gee, oh wow! And the wheel is turning, the turning of the wheel, the Wheel of Fortune. Oh my!"

"Come on. Come on," the guy yelled. "What's happening? What's going on over there?"

"Sir, what was your name?" Suddenly I seemed cooperative and willing to offer him some answers.

"Dougy. My name's Dougy."

"Well, Doughy, I mean Dougy, I'm not sure how—I mean, well—I don't know how to bring this up. But the cards indicate some peculiar energies surrounding you. Actually Dougy, they are emotional energies that are coming from inside you."

I paused.

He snorted, "What? What in the hell are you talking about? What kind of emotions?"

I ignored his question and continued. "Oh, and now I'm sensing sounds, yes, yes, musical sounds that are *surrounding* you. So there is inner stuff and outer stuff. Both at the same time."

His disposition shifted and the sound of his voice was younger, less gruff. "What kind of sounds?"

"I should explain, Dougy, that I'm *not* a clairvoyant. I'm more of a stereo-audio-voyant."

"A what? What in the hell is that?"

"Well, it means that I'm not seeing things about you or your future, but I'm *hearing* things. And when I tune in to your aura I can hear Judy Garland songs. It's the damnedest thing. Yes, Judy Garland, and—oh my God, wait a second. Yep, there's Barbra Streisand coming in from the left channel. It's amazing. Simply amazing. Judy on the right. Babs on the left. And Doug, they sound fantastic!"

I pictured a bewildered look on his face when he asked, "What in the hell does that have to do with anything? What does it mean? Hurry, what does it mean?"

"Um, well, I know you are concerned about the time, so I'll just say this the quickest way I can. I see deep repressed longings beginning to surface in your life. So let me just ask you: Dougy, have you taken the time to acknowledge your latent homosexual feelings? Your sexual fantasies about being with another man? These are the longings that you'll be having in the future."

The silence on the other end of the phone was screaming. And then *he* screamed, "What in the fuck are you talking about?! I'm calling about getting laid and you're talking some queer shit. This is a rip-off!"

I paused for a long time, cleared my throat, and beamed a big smile. And even though she'd never hear about it, I was happy for the "downtown chick."

"I bet you're relieved to finally have this out in the open, aren't you, Dougy?"

Click. Dial tone.

Helen Got Her Gun

I was ready to call it a night. My high jinks with Dougy seemed a great way to close the early morning on an affirmative note. I was ready for bed. But the phone was ringing again. My immediate reaction was instinctual: just unplug the phone mid-ring and lose the money. But I felt compelled to answer.

Helen was calling from New York. Obviously drunk, she was droning on about some guy that she loved who had passed out on her living-room couch. He was drunk too. She said that she knew she shouldn't love him as much as she did because he was "an abusive bastard" and yet, despite all of her love, she was afraid for her life.

"He threatened me with a knife over the weekend," she admitted.

When I heard this, I interrupted her story and jumped into action. I didn't read her cards—I just did a Barbara De Angelis and said, "Get out of that relationship. Now! Pronto!"

I heard a dull thumping and next crackly static, and then, right when I thought she'd hung up, she was back on the line. I asked her what had happened and she told me she was in her garage, in her car, hiding on the floor behind the back seat, holding a bottle of vodka in one hand and a gun *and* a cellular phone in the other. She had lost her grip on the gun and the phone had tumbled onto the floor alongside her.

I remember that my eyes felt very large and I thought to myself, "Oh geez, now she's going to want suicide counseling." It was half past two in the morning and I knew I couldn't leave her in a lurch.

I said, "Helen." Silence. And then I yelled, "Helen! Helen! Can you hear me?"

She mumbled something about the Lord and said, "I don't want to do it. I just can't do it. I know I . . ."

"Helen," I interrupted. "Just put the gun down and let me give you an 800 number for the suicide hot line. I want you to call them. It's free. I don't want you wasting your money talking to me."

There was a creepy, dead-zone pause, and I was doodling wildly on a pad in front of me. And then Helen let out a big hoot followed by a wild rattle of smokers-cough and laughter mixed together.

"Honey, I'm not going to kill myself. I'm trying to talk myself outa going in that house and killing *him*. That bastard is going to pay for . . ." And on and on she went.

I just hung on the line and let her get out all of her frustrations—about forty dollars worth. Toward the end of the call she told me how much better she felt. And so I felt better. I let out a long sigh and told Helen that I had to go because it was way too late. She understood and said, "God bless you, darlin'. This has been very revealing." And I was off to bed.

I knew in my heart she wouldn't kill the guy.

Well, maybe not.

10
Flesh and Blood or Electricity and Anonymity

The telephone is a good way to talk to people
without having to offer them a drink.
FRAN LEBOWITZ

Eventually, with much celebration, I escaped from the graveyard shift. And I did this by remaining consistent, which meant logging on to the lines religiously and working a predetermined amount of hours. Consequently, my average built up and I moved happily up the network's priority ladder. But this sort of discipline was a stretch for me, because a phone psychic's central temptation is procrastination—which, the few times I made the mistake, proved Baudelaire's bromide: "In putting off what one has to do, one runs the risk of never being able to do it." In my case, the culprit isn't capability. I just flat out refuse to work. Three hours a day on the phones is above and beyond the call of duty for me. The thought of pulling a six-hour shift conjures visions of hari-kari. I'm always explaining to friends how an hour on the phones is the equivalent of three hours at their jobs. Phone psychics are paid strictly by the minute, which doesn't include chats at the water cooler, stealing office supplies, or lengthy makeup applications in the bathroom.

To escape the midnight shift, I also had to work out small compromises with my ethics. Initially, after I'd answer a call, I'd try to determine, before the reading began, if the caller should be paying four dollars a minute to talk to me or not. Were they on welfare, unemployed, or mentally unstable? My conscience was constantly niggling me until I finally stopped questioning. I had to trust that if someone was calling, then they needed to talk. And so I talked and listened. This attitude shift also helped ensure that my call average was good and that our refrigerator was well stocked.

The Real Challenge

The biggest adjustment I've had to make as a phone psychic is the absence of physical presence. For years I'd become accustomed to working face-to-face with my clients. But on the phones there isn't any visual detail. Everything is held within the imagination. And that can be a frightening place to be when you depend on the sound of a voice to define your ground.

In one of his technical papers, Freud wrote about how the secrets of the analytic patients leak out from every pore without their knowledge. As a counselor I rely upon those clues tremendously. When a client sits across from me there is a world of presence to read from. The way they shift in their chair or flip their hair, the way their eyes drop or slide off to the side when asked a difficult question—none of those clues are available when I'm on the phone. I get a voice, and that's it. Or is it?

The high priest of popular culture, Marshall McLuhan, defined the telephone as "a participant form that demands a partner, with all the intensity of electric polarity." This explains why we've become a nation of "screeners," letting our answering machines intervene and prolong our option to share or withhold. A ringing phone is a pressing demand from the outside world to connect and participate.

This "electronic meeting," according to McLuhan, demands "maximum attention," where all of the senses "rally to strengthen the weak sound of the phone." McLuhan considered this demand to concentrate to be an instinctual response, and he recommended that teachers use the telephone to instruct individuals with short attention spans or learning disorders.

For the same reasons, counseling on a psychic line creates wonderful opportunities for an intense, instantaneous rapport—for cogent exchange intensified by the powers of divination. This "electronic polarity" creates a paradoxical blend of conditions for the caller: a strong emotional link and focus of attention supported by the safety and comfortability of anonymity.

I remember reading an interview in which Yoko Ono explained how talking on the phone allowed her to reveal her emotions much more quickly than if she were meeting with someone face-to-face. I couldn't agree more. Conversing with hundreds of people each month, in short ten- or twenty-minute sessions, proves how anonymity enhances the caller's courage. I'm always amazed at how the caller's vulnerability runs neck and neck with intrepid daring. In dialing the phone they're preparing to make a confessional blitzkrieg. It's all or nothing, and the psychic who answers the call had better be prepared for the arrival of the troops.

Over the years, I've noticed how most of the clients who've come to me for astrological consultations will relax and reveal psychological material that would take months for a psychiatrist to excavate. And for many of my callers, the telephone arrangement, with its high per-minute cost and its anonymity, quadruples the speed of their "opening up" process. Within minutes they'll dart straight to the heart of whatever sheltered secret or doubt is plaguing them.

Often their urgency is unnerving. It's similar to the surprise you get when a shaken stranger comes rushing toward you on a busy sidewalk, clearly intent on getting your attention. You just know that their request is going to be unusual. Maybe their friend is pinned under a car somewhere and they want you to help pull the poor soul out. This intense immediacy isn't always easy to work with. Initially, I felt challenged and ill-prepared, but eventually I came to honor the caller's courage and learned how to meet their force with an equally strong willingness to engage.

Psychics or Psychiatrists?

Why do people reveal so much more, so quickly, to a psychic than they would to a therapist or family counselor? My theory is that most people don't go to therapists or psychiatrists. Often discourse with a psychic is the first opportunity a caller has had to broach subjects they've avoided or denied. I also think that deep down most people don't really believe in astrology and the tarot the same way they "believe" in psychotherapy. And despite all the mental-health experts they've watched on the Ricki Lake show, a good portion of our society still equates psychotherapy with being crazy or dysfunctional.

The psychic print ads and infomercials all carry the same disclaimer: "For entertainment purposes only." Entertainment usually means something fun, and fun usually means something safe. And feeling safe, as a qualifier for trust, is ultimately what all of those shrinks and social workers have been trained to nurture in their clients. Personally, I prefer the opportunities afforded by my electronic-analyst's couch: a fun, energized, instantaneous rapport that fosters the caller's spirit of inquiry.

Scientifically we claim to understand the restorative power of healing, but do we? Healing is alchemical, invisible, and mysterious. And yet, what is easily identifiable about the healing experience is the necessity for participation and exchange. Even a cut finger requires the loving application of a Band-Aid. So too the discomforts of the heart, mind, and soul. As a phone psychic, I've experienced AT&T's "Reach out and touch someone" slogan as a very real phenomenon. My energized conversations with a diverse group of curious souls repeatedly prove how a little attention, imagination, and heart can help mend and restore.

11
The Heart of the Matter

God created Man because he enjoys stories.

YIDDISH PROVERB

"This bitch is gonna tell you some shit. I'm serious girl—just let her do the talking and you're gonna really hear some shit tonight." This advice came from one woman speaking over the phone to another. They were waiting on the same line but at different extensions.

Every call I answer begins with a "whisper code," a short, three-second prerecorded voice that lets me know what special division the caller selected for the reading. Because many networks offer specialty psychics, customers can pick from different keypad options like "Choose 1 for Psychic Romance," "Choose 2 for Money Magic," and "Choose 3 for Reincarnation Replay." Should an operator answer during the middle of the prompt, the caller can't hear the psychic's arrival. This is what happened with the two women waiting for the "bitch" to come on the line.

"I'm telling you, I am going to jump all over his shit if he's been lying. I can't deal with it anymore." And then her girlfriend let out a loud "Mmmm-hmmm, I hear you girl. Just wait."

"So when is she going to answer?"

"Just wait, just wait."

Too curious to not eavesdrop, I let them wait. Obviously, the woman promoting the call had already received a reading several minutes before from the "bitch" psychic. She was calling again, this time for her friend, using the operator's extension number. But it is rare to hang up, redial, and reach the same psychic again. Usually a redial will be forwarded to another operator—in this case, me. I hit the mute button on my phone and waited for their conversation to resume.

"Well, what in the hell is happening? Where is she?"

"She'll get on—just wait."

The friend cautiously asked, "Are you going to ask her about the gonorrhea thing you're worried about?"

"I don't know. Should I?"

"Maybe you'd better."

"No, I just want to know if he's cheating. I want to hear the story about that bullshit."

A couple of minutes ticked by. Not wanting to cheat the woman who should have been calling an STD clinic instead of an electronic oracle, I made my appearance on the line, explained how their call had been rerouted, and before requesting a birth date, wrote in the margin of my notebook, "I want to hear the story."

"I'm seeing two words," I mysteriously offered.

"What two words? What do you mean?" asked Jeannie, who was receiving the reading. She was being coached by Channele.

"Two words floating in the field of vision."

"Field of vision? Is that like the field of dreams or something?" Jeannie inquired.

"No, two *words* in front of my eyes. The words are *sex* and *doctor*. Do you have any idea what that means?"

Channele laughed. Jeannie became excited: "Oh, he is good, girl. He is *real* good." I feigned curiosity—but Jeannie wasn't telling.

"So, let's move into the love-connection stuff," Channele offered.

"Yeah, I wanna know something about Reggie, my boyfriend." Jeannie sounded excited and nervous. "What do you see going down with him? What's he up to right now. I wanna hear *his* story."

I delivered my standard Proxy Disclaimer and explained how I can't invade another person's force field to cull specific facts but how, reading by proxy, the cards usually pick up the *caller's* unconscious knowledge of the situation.

"Yeah, yeah, whatever," Jeannie agreed.

The consultation spiraled into a forty-minute mix of shock, laughter, declarations of revenge (Reggie wasn't showing up so hot in this reading), quelled anger, and finally Jeannie's resolve to confront Reggie openly.

But Jeannie, not satisfied with the tarot's stream of disappointing imagery and revelations, kept pushing for "one more reading, one more reading. I've got to know how he really feels about me." I advised her that we should stick to what we'd already discovered.

"OK, so you're telling me what I already know. But does he love me—that's what I've *got* to know? Does he love me?"

"Oh God," I thought to myself. For the last thirty minutes I'd listened to Jeannie detail how Reggie had been caught cheating on her—with not one but two different women, had ditched his first wife, and had paid no child support for his three kids. And so far the only thing he'd given her was the clap.

But I was familiar with this heartbreaking "does so-and-so love me?" query. It's one of the most frequently asked questions on the lines. And like a pat question, I had a standard response.

"Yes, Jeannie, he does love you, but fate seems to be pulling him in another direction—away from you."

Finally, she popped.

"It's time we had it out," Jeannie announced. "I'm going to see him tomorrow, tell him what I know about his bullshit. And the truth is gonna set me free."

Channele agreed. I agreed. We hung up. I logged off. Done. Kaput.

I released a long sigh, relieved to be finished for the night, but I was pensive and perplexed. I'd been plugged into America's psychic power grid for seven months, and I was beginning to feel the repercussions. What began as a novel enterprise—an enlivening spark—now felt like a redundant short-circuit. Despite my psychological spins with the tarot and astrology, the callers expected visions and futurescapes—

and frequently wanted these fantasies to corroborate their delusions. Ethically I refused to comply. In my heart I was a counselor, not a fortune-teller. And yet the rent was due.

I looked at my notebook again. The sentence "I want to hear the story" levitated off the page and accompanied me to bed. Appropriately enough, a lengthy dream ensued:

I was a tour guide in a large art museum. Instead of a normal-sized group of tourists, I'd been mistakenly assigned hundreds of individuals, and it was up to me to entertain each and every one of them throughout the excursion and to hold the entire group's attention as well. I would stop before each painting, and rather than explain historical facts, I would make up fantastic stories about its content. I would assign names to the characters or animals in the painting and spin colorful tales and parables. The raconteur in me was running full throttle. When I awoke the next morning, I knew exactly what I needed to do to rejuvenate my efforts on the phone.

Love Toys

Carol from South Carolina was my first call of the evening. She and her husband were locked in a sexless marriage. For Tony, the relationship was fine, or so Carol said. He was loyal, a hard worker, and paid all the bills. As their marriage progressed into its third year, Tony had begun to hold Carol in a surrogate-mother position. What did the future hold for her?

"Well, have you considered professional counseling?" I inquired.

"Oh, no. Tony would never go for something like that. He's too old-fashioned," she answered firmly.

"Have you thought about counseling for yourself?" I countered.

"I don't think Tony would understand."

"Do you feel like the marriage is worth saving?" I asked. "Is there a lot of love between the two of you still?"

"Yes, I guess so," she assured me. "Tony is a wonderful provider. It's just that I find myself wondering why we aren't having relations with each other."

A lot of my callers from the South substitute the word *relations* for, well, *sexual intimacy*. I thought it was charming.

I turned my attention to her tarot spread. The Lovers card was first, which indicated an important decision. Second was the Seven of Cups, meaning that Carol's imagination would offer a key. And above, not surprisingly, was the Devil, representing Carol's hearty libido. The imagery made me feel bold. I offered, "Well, Carol, have you thought about taking a lover?"

"What?" she gasped.

That wasn't going to work. I shifted strategies. "Have you ever fantasized about another man?"

She let out a tiny giggle. "Oh, maybe once I did. Last month at my sister's wedding I saw a really cute guy who was a couple of years younger than me. But I could never do that to Tony."

I moved forward. "I can see here, Carol, that you need to find some kind of outlet for your fantasy life. Fantasy and sexuality go hand in hand, you know. Maybe you could work on this approach in your relationship."

"Oh, no. Tony wouldn't like that."

"Well, how about exploring your own fantasy life?" I asked.

Dead air.

"Are you there, Carol?" I inquired.

"Yes," a timid voice answered.

"Do you think you could allow yourself to have a little excitement with your imagination?"

"I guess so, but what do I do?"

I decided to tell the story.

"Carol, I'm getting a vision. I see a young woman with dark hair. She's walking along the edge of a beautiful lake. There are swans in the lake and the air is very cool. She feels a deep contentment in her heart. As she continues to move along the shore, clouds begin to appear. The air becomes chilly. The swans disappear and rain begins to fall. She needs to take shelter. And so she retreats into a millhouse that she discovers on the edge of a nearby river. Now, this millhouse is owned by an industrious man. When she knocks at the door, he offers her shelter."

I asked Carol if she could picture this fellow and tell me what he was like.

"He's friendly. I do like him. His eyes are very sweet. And he's very calm—sort of cool toward me."

I continued, "So, she enters the millhouse, and what does she discover? What does she find?"

She answered immediately, "A broom and a dustpan, and she starts sweeping. The place is just a mess. I don't think anyone has cleaned up in there in a long time."

"So she sweeps and sweeps and cleans and cleans. And after a while she forgets about the peace of mind she felt outside when she was walking around the lake. And you know what? In a flash, three years have passed, and she is still sweeping and cleaning."

"Oh, this is awful. Bring her back outside, into the sun."

"I don't think I can, Carol. For some reason she feels the need to stay in the millhouse. But maybe that's not such a bad thing. Let me go further with the story and see what I can see. Should I?"

"Yes, yes. Keep going."

"It's another sunny day. There is a gentle wind. Again, she is cleaning the millhouse. But this time she discovers some loose planks in the wooden floor. She hesitates, but her curiosity is strong. She pries open the planks and discovers an elegantly bound book. Do you know what this book is about, Carol?"

"I can't imagine."

"Well, try. Try to imagine."

"I don't know. Tell me."

"It is a pillow book. You've heard of Japanese pillow books, haven't you?"

"Why, yes, I have. But what are they?"

"Books that detail the many ways a couple can make love. They show pictures of . . ."

"But what does this have to do with me? What does the vision mean?"

"I see you purchasing some adult magazines or maybe some steamy erotica. As you are reading the magazine you come across an advertisement for some adult novelty items, objects you can order through the mail. You place an order with the company and discover that you really like the adult toys when they finally arrive in the mail."

Again there was vacant silence on the other end of the phone. And then suddenly she asked, "What kind of adult toys are they?"

I thought to myself, "Do I really need to broach the subject of dildos on a psychic line?" I decided against it.

"Well, why don't you just start with the magazine and then see what comes up? See if you actually like the erotica first, and then you can explore the other part of this story."

"OK, that's what I will do." And then she added, "Do you think I am ready for this right now?"

"Oh yes," I said, "definitely. This fantasy is just waiting to happen."

Clues and Cues

The story I devised from the simple images of Carol's tarot reading might seem corny if taken out of context, but it *was* effective. Would reading the pillow book prompt a return to her autonomous world, outside, beside the lake? Or would the keeper of the mill begin to respond differently to his imaginative partner? I'd probably never know.

Regardless, this simple imaginary excursion provided a link. I don't think Carol would have stayed on the phone one second past the mention of "adult novelty items" if I hadn't prefaced my recommendation with the story. Stories, daydreams, and fairy tales can act as a mediating device between the person we are right now and the ideal we only vaguely sense ourselves becoming. I believe that the psyche is continually offering us clues. And unless we slow down and let ourselves feel our desires, we'll miss the clues and cues that point the way.

What We Want, Why We Don't Get It, and How We Might

In his book *Carnival Culture*, James B. Twitchell writes, "In many respects popular culture resembles a secular religion promising release, not in the next world, but in this one. Wishes are fulfilled, not later, but *now*. Gratification is instant because for the first time it can be. There is so much to look at, so much to see."

But despite the glut of films, television shows, videos, computer games, and theme parks, there seems to be more titillation than release, and certainly not enough of either to quell the source of our longing. What we really want is a personal connection with the mythic level of life, something beyond sitting back and watching another special-effects-driven movie or reading a cheesy romance novel. As appetizers, those distractions are fine, but many of us are hankering for the full meal.

Spiritual pundits complain about the consumer machinery that keeps us greedy for more and more titillation and distraction. But I'm intrigued with how we keep gorging ourselves, how we keep moving feverishly toward entertainment overload, as if we're hoping that after a bad case of indigestion—and a gigantic, collective belch—the values which motivate and guide our fantasies might be revealed. But I'm not one of those conspiracy theorists who blame modern culture for our spiritual weakness. The outer world shifts in accordance to the movements within our hearts and souls. As we change internally, so do the products we purchase and the diversions we seek.

So our predicament is an internal, private affair—and not the simplest to remedy. We each carry within our unconscious a backlog of childhood parental rules, societal pressures, and religious morals that seriously mitigate our instinct to desire, wish, and dream. Freud called this oppressive force the superego. And it's the superego's function to keep the status quo in place by asserting its dream-squelching prohibitions. Almost every individual with whom I converse talks about struggling with this internal censoring agent. Each conversation, regardless of content, is fueled by the caller's difficulty in allowing themselves to picture their life in a new light. Many people feel embarrassed or frightened to act on their desire to live differently.

It's my job, as a mystical tour guide, to mirror the magical world of stories and fantasies within my callers' imaginations. I'm like a good friend or sibling who doesn't criticize, scold, dent, or tamper with the dream. I might provide reality checks, but only as a way to support a more detailed kind of dreaming. Often I'm the medicine man who admits his shortcomings and refers the caller to his competition: a good shrink or family counselor. I provide hints to help the caller solve the mystery, the mystery that is in their heart.

My methods vary, depending on the caller's issues and how much latitude they'll grant me to play. Often I keep it simple and ask, "If one thing could be different for you, right now, what would it be? Tell me about it." And then I'll follow their answer with a colorful narrative culled from their horoscope or spread of cards. If the caller is willing, I'll read poetry from Kabir or prayers from Christian mystics. I'll paint futuristic visions from the clues and cues I've collected throughout our conversation. I'll avidly promote the seeking of assistance from a Higher Power and carefully explain how we need allies in life to guide us through our next experience or challenge.

One of my favorite tactics is making lists. I consider list making the equivalent of doing a Rorschach inkblot test without the inkblots. It's uncomplicated yet magical. A list is like a poem. And lists can reveal much about the list maker. A book's table of contents, items that we shop for, things you find in the rubbish, directions for a scavenger hunt, an inventory of your dreams from the month of May, a movie theater's marquee, things you find in a woman's purse, your New Year's resolutions—all of these are different kinds of giveaways.

Shortly into the consultation I will ask the caller to play "Let's Make a List." I'll interrupt their litany of complaints and say, "Stop. Right now: Give me a list!"

They'll usually ask, "What do you mean?"

And I'll respond, "Just give me a list, any kind of list—right off the top of your head. Right now." And then the child in them will understand—and out rolls their list. It can be a list of anything: favorite foods, colors, hobbies, books, sports, vacation spots, or artists, actors, or musicians—or any of these subjects combined.

List making transports us to the inner sanctum of our heart. We usually associate lists with things that we are fond of or desire or wish to accomplish. This benign little exercise does wonders to banish the superego long enough for the heart's door to open and reveal its contents.

Many of us have forgotten what it is we really want. And there's nothing more engaging and revealing than a loving gaze at the contents of our hearts. A simple appraisal can help us remember. And when we remember, we can relax and reconnect with our ability to generate our own dreams and stories. I prefer working with folks this way. Even when callers feel distanced from what they want and need, I know that with a little assistance and magic, they're a few short steps away from the heart of the matter.

PART TWO

But Enough about Me—Here's the Meaning of Life

12
The "Real" Thing

Many a time I have wanted to stop talking and
find out what I really believed.
WALTER LIPPMAN

To be honest, I've never thought of myself as a very good fortune-teller. I'll attempt to part the veil and take a peek into tomorrow land, but my list of accurate, earth-shattering predictions is about as long as my little finger. Whoop-de-do—call the *National Enquirer*.

Instead, I consider myself a pragmatic mystic, someone who enjoys being wowed by the wonder of the here and now while sewing a button on a shirt. Sure, I can toy with probabilities, but the weight of my magical aptitude and acuity rests in the present—and extends no further than what's for lunch this afternoon. So when people call to discuss the future of their love longings, undulating bank account, or job prospects, they discover I'm not the Wizard of Oz. I'm just the man behind the curtain. And yet I do offer them something worthwhile. In fact, it's pretty important: I've cracked the future code.

This future thing is a paradox. We worry about the future when it's the present to which we should give our attention. Because we've forgotten how to appreciate the here and now, we feel that something is missing in the present, so we're easily convinced that what we really need is a new lover, a bigger car, a new pair of Nikes, and more channels on our television. But what's really missing is the proper evaluation of what's missing. And what is really missing is a vital relationship with ourselves—our hidden self, the "real" you and me, the essential part within each of us.

When people call, I make a subtle effort to address their secret self. Our dialogue might involve the future, but the underlying motif I support is the importance of finding a way back to what is real and true within each person—a homecoming of sorts, a way to reacquaint themselves with what's true and real about who they really are in the present. And for all of us, this relationship with our real self is the most fascinating subject in the world.

It's Got to Be Real

Our culture's obsession with the idyll of the real is a by-product of our awareness that nothing lasts. Consequently, we search for what is permanent and secure.

We want the people in our life to be "real." When we fall in love, we hope it's the "real thing" we'll land in. We want products that are "real, 100 percent natural," and the radio is full of songs conveying longing for "real" people, places, and things.

Is this clamoring a delusion? I don't think so. We're sensing the difference between the true and the false in life. Many spiritual and psychological schools of thought distinguish between what is genuine in a person and what is false. The false part is the personality, from the Greek word *persona,* which means "mask." The real part is the essential self, the true heart and soul of a person. And with a little assistance we can use our intuition, like a Geiger counter, to sift through the dross in search of the missing gold that is our secret self.

We all have a hidden self, but expressing its realness is difficult. There's little support for this quest in our culture's drive to succeed and survive. The real self is a mystery, as mysterious as life itself. It's beyond definition. And yet this real self in each of us wants to define and actualize its gifts, show its colors, and sing its song—to make the real real. We're each waiting for the day when our real selves will come forward to play in the world instead of hanging out in the background, behind the masks.

Once the real self is acknowledged, we want to know more. And, more importantly, we want to participate and nurture our relationship with what's real. We can do this by exploring subjects like spirituality, meditation, psychology, astrology, the tarot, and mystical inquiry. Wondering about the real self, wanting definition and insight about its nature, and finding ways to express its presence all mark the beginning of the process of awakening. And awakening, although arduous at times, begins to fulfill our soul's deepest desire to be real.

Initially, the real self communicates to us in symbols or codes, not literal messages, so we need to pay attention. The message is subtle, and it usually arrives as a deep, ineffable longing, a feeling I call the mystical impulse.

Metaphysical systems, psychic arts, myths, fairy tales, and dreams are timeless and remain firmly rooted within our imagination. We're enamored with otherworldly and make-believe stories because our real self often feels magical yet distanced, under our skin yet invisible.

My aim is to discuss these subjects lightly and without analyzing their mystery and allure. I can't explain how or why magic, astrology, and divination actually work. But we *can* inquire into their mysteries. Inquiry is one of the central ways in which the real self begins to be revealed. When we inquire, we are just checking things out. We look without having preconceptions about what we are going to find. We're just enjoying the ride.

Psychics: What's Not in a Name

I'm not a psychic in the traditional sense of the word. I've never solved an unsolved mystery, bent a spoon in half with my over-amped telekinetic powers, or channeled the spirit of a grizzled biblical prophet. I'm a *telephone psychic*, a friendly, empathetic ear on the other end of the line who works with insight and intuition. I can read astrological charts and synthesize the symbols from a spread of tarot cards. I'm a sensitive guy—an intuitive person who can sense what is going on with a person by the sound of their voice and the stories they tell me. Now, add a dash of metaphor, a little chutzpah, some intuitive creativity, a mixing of the cards, and—voilà—a psychic is born. That's about it. So you might be psychic too.

The Secret Psychic Quiz

1. Think about a person you really like. (Come on, let's play. Don't just plow through the words here.)
2. Now, imagine this person as a flower.
3. Ask yourself, What kind of flower is it? Is it on a bush, or standing alone, or in a pot? What color is it? Is the flower open or is it still a bud? Does it have leaves? Does it have thorns? Let your imagination paint as many details as it can.

You've just constructed a symbol in your mind and imagination that represents your friend. It's like a visual poem. The feelings and sensations you experienced while compiling your image are important clues that tell you intuitive information. If the flower is open, the person is open. If you picture a bud, perhaps they're beginning something. Thorns might indicate defensiveness. If it's a single flower, your friend might feel lonely or isolated—or perhaps solitude is appropriate right now. You can actually feel the person within the image. This is exactly the way I operate when I talk to people. I concentrate on a subject, intuit an image, and then circuit my impressions through my imagination to deliver a reading.

It's simple, isn't it?

Reviving the Feminine

Our culture tends to minimize paranormal professions, so there isn't much support for anyone feeling a psychic urge. Imagine a child telling her father, "Dad, I want to be a numerologist when I grow up," and the dad saying, "Sure! Great! Let me take the money I set aside for your college education and find you a good occultist."

Depending on one's gender, temperament, and upbringing, it's either confirming or disturbing to acknowledge one's psychic gifts. Some individuals do so easily, and they might attend a psychic school to foster their sensitivity and to learn how to honor their hunches, intuitions, dreams, and visions. Others will master subjects like astrology or the tarot—systems of thought that strengthen the intuition's ability to work with images and symbols.

Sometimes a person's psychic awareness might be hidden or avoided. Men, especially, can have a hard time when their sensitivity to seemingly irrational impressions begins to impinge on their lives. These psychic proclivities might be considered embarrassing or unmanly.

Psychics, astrologers, tarot readers, intuitives—all of these belong to the archetype of the feminine, and this explains why our culture, and some of those aforementioned men, have a hard time accepting the viability of intuitive arts. Sociologically speaking, feminine ways of perception and expression are not honored and promoted the same way masculine principles are upheld. Because survival and security are such compelling drives, the logical, rational, practical approach holds precedence. But this is starting to change. The oppression of the feminine realm is beginning to lift, and these intuitive, reflective, and imaginative qualities are beginning to reassert themselves into everyday life. Maybe this is why thousands of people consult with psychics every day.

The Anatomy of a Psychic

I've noticed certain commonalities among psychics. For instance, most of my metaphysical friends share a deep, existential questioning toward life. And many feel dissatisfied with the "surface" level of what our culture has to offer—the shapes, forms, structures, rules, roles, and institutions that our society deems valuable and worthy of pursuit. Like myself, they struggle with integrating their spiritual lives into the concerns of everyday living, with finding a way to live in the real world while still honoring their mystical impulses. It's not an easy task.

The Sufis describe this challenge as one of being "in the world but not of it." Whenever we forgo the safety of a conventional life we need to find ways to honor the spiritual without turning our back on the world we live in.

Exploring magic and the rituals of divination can expand our capacity to be present and yet transcendent. To trust the flow of unseen currents. To follow the lead of our real self. And yet, contrary to conventional ways of thinking, magic and divination ground us firmly in the present moment. Both subjects are a perfect blend of the simplistic and the extraordinary.

Omnipresent Magic

When we make a wish, repeat an affirmation, or say a prayer, we are eliciting a magical act. And when we cross our fingers, knock on wood, or light a candle for a friend who is having a difficult time, we are doing a ritual to conjure a magical intervention.

Imagine this: It's late in the afternoon. You decide to take a stroll along the beach. You lose track of time. The next thing you know you're standing very still on the shoreline, watching a glorious sunset unleash brilliant blends of orange, red, and yellow light across the horizon. You sense an awe-inspiring stillness throughout your body, and your heart feels a powerful upwelling of love and gratitude. You're under a magical spell. Although your mind may want to trivialize or discredit your experience, it is, in fact, a potent, magic moment in which your mind has moved aside and your real self has asserted its presence.

A meaningful book, a spectacular painting, a visit to a temple or church—each can generate a sense of magic. Some writers are renowned for their ability to weave magical spells with their poems and move the reader into a state filled with wondrous associations.

Magic can inspire us, enthuse us, and crack open even the hardest shell. By the way, the word *enthusiasm* means "possessed by God."

The Technology of Intuition

"Common sense" is common only because it's the way most us approach the process of decision making. Practical thinking means coloring within the lines and solving problems the way everyone else solves problems. So our solutions are probably the same old solutions everyone else comes up with—and probably aren't solutions at all but just another form of the same old problem. Society places tremendous pressure on us to discern and discriminate correctly. The motto "Choose wisely" haunts us like an ominous decree from a childhood fairy tale. So we never give ourselves much latitude to think and plan in a creative, original way.

If life were predictable, our "common sense" would be a fine decision-making process. We could approach everything like a science. But life is riddled with unexpected twists and turns and moments of intense unknowing. This is where divination enters the picture. Divination offers us alternative ways to choose, discern, and discriminate—magical ways. In an uncertain world, divination is the surest way we have of maintaining a link with the mysterious way in which life unfolds.

Here's Webster's definition of *divination*: "The art or practice that seeks to foresee or foretell future events or discover hidden knowledge usually by the interpretation of omens or by the aid of supernatural powers." And the dictionary's second definition defines those supernatural powers: "Unusual insight, intuitive perception." What's revealing is the state of mind alluded to in the latter definition. We need a state of openness and quietude to access "hidden knowledge."

Initially, divination was an instinctual reaction to uncertainty. When the gap between the conscious and unconscious closes, divination naturally occurs. As it exists today, divination is a vestige from a time when the soul was effortlessly in synch with the external world.

Suppose you've been fired from your job and have no prospects. What should you do next? Well, you could go immediately into mental overdrive, worrying and furiously planning your next move. Or you could remain calm, turning your attention to your intuition, lingering to apprehend the unknown, and waiting to see what is revealed. It comes either internally from your unconscious, perhaps through a dream or your active imagination, or from the world around you, through an omen or some synchronistic event.

Some of you might choose to consult an astrologer or tarot reader, using *their* intuitive skills in lieu of your own. Regardless, what you're doing is divining. It's not about the future so much as it's about *yourself*. Fortune-telling really has to do with prognostication. But divination is an interior assessment of our being and how our being is linked and relating to the outside world.

When we divine, we create a pause, a quiet moment of contemplation that allows divine intervention to point the way. And this direction could involve your future—your plans, expectations, and direction. Or surprisingly enough, it could involve your past, revealing unresolved fears and doubts—issues you must confront in order to allow for a new berth of passage. And then again, divination might offer no direction at all. You must wait in the stillness of the present moment, suspended yet watchful, paying attention to your circumstances to deliver the key you are searching for.

Reality Check

Let's talk about reality for a minute. I like to think of reality as an actual force, a living thing—a force that animates and contains everything in life. Reality is the universe humming. If we feel out of alignment with this force, we begin to atrophy and life becomes dull and dead. Divination can help us reconfigure our internal homing device and reconnect to the hum and flow of the universe. In short, divination is a form of active meditation, a way of creating a channel for reality to display its omniscience.

We can never know for certain what the future portends. But divination invites us to relax, settle into the present moment, and discover guidance from the world of dreams and omens, from the magic of synchronized events. Guidance can also arrive in the conscious world through a movie you see on television, a letter that arrives in the mail, or a casual comment made by a friend. We might dismiss this way of thinking as nonsensical, superstitious, or impractical. But that's the point! Divination strikes a counterpoint to the limiting dictates of common sense and rationality.

Practical thinking is fine for making sure you catch your bus on time. But as a creative, vibrant way to enter the flow of life, it's limiting. This is especially true in moments of disruption, crisis, and turmoil. But reality assumes many faces, and even chaos and disorder have their function. Often disruptions point the way to a larger, more creative way of living. And divination can help us weather those periods with grace and trust.

Herman Hesse said, "Chaos demands to be recognized and experienced before letting itself be converted into a new order." Divination, especially when self-practiced, creates a space through which a natural and gradual process, a new order, can unfold. And if we practice divination regularly, we'll discover a confidence and faith not possible from our commonsense approach to living.

Knowing our direction is not as important as having a *sense of fusion* with the very force that supports and propels our direction. This implies feeling the vitality and open-ended nature of reality, void of any distinct aim or outcome. Divination summons a state of mind that reminds us of our relationship and interconnectedness with everything and everyone around us. And when we can really sense and feel this connection we're able to relax and align ourselves with the intention of our real self. Intention is usually experienced through our enthusiasm and passion, and as most of us can attest, passion is what propels us forward toward the next unknown place in our life.

Fortune-Telling, Fortune-Mirroring

"So what are you doing right now?"

Marsha was calling from Connecticut, and she had an important question.

"I want to know how you're going to see the future. Are you going into a trance or something?"

"No, nothing like that, Marsha."

"Well, what's up, honey? Whatcha doing over there in Seattle?"

I was preparing to access her story and provide her with a "reading." She wanted to know about her future with a guy named Larry.

"I'm going for my tarot cards," I explained. "And now I'm going to do some mixing."

"That sounds neat," Marsha said.

I kept shuffling, still in divination mode. Shuffling, still shuffling. *Ping*. The oven timer went off in my head, the cake was done, shuffling could stop, parallel universes had intermingled. I laid out the cards.

Her tarot spread was a burst of intense emotion. The bright yellows and greens of the Empress card dominated the center. I could sense Marsha's enthusiasm and sincerity. But the next card, which checks the first, was the Two of Swords, a symbol of equilibrium, perhaps indecision and doubt, and the colors were gray and a somber blue—a cautious condition, and not a state of mind associated with the Empress's intrinsic zestfulness. This was an ambivalent Empress.

A picture came to my mind: Marsha and Larry sitting down for candlelit dinner. But no one was eating—their mood was pensive, and Marsha had picked up the menu again, covering her face while she considered other choices. Like the figure depicted in the Two of Swords, Marsha was weighing, assessing the relationship cautiously. I sensed she'd known Larry for a long time. I asked her.

"Yeah, I've known Larry for two years now. Why?"

"Because I think you're uncertain about Larry's history, his past. Something's bugging you. Disrupting your romantic feelings. Are you hesitant for some reason?"

"Well, yes. He's married."

I was still in divination mode but preparing to flip into the tricky art of fortune-telling, or fortune-mirroring, as I call it. I glanced at the cards again, studying the "final outcome" position. There was the Eight of Cups, an emblem that mirrored my vision of Marsha searching for other items on the menu. The Eight of Cups's moody picture of a man turning away from his collection of valuable cups to assume a new quest is both enlivening and melancholic. What's wrong with the treasure he's already collected? Well, in Marsha's case, she'd collected two years worth of disappointments and broken promises. Surely it was time to move on. Or was it? And if so, to where? To what? Those were secrets even Nostradamus couldn't crack. But Marsha could.

"I'm getting a feeling of movement. Where are you heading, Marsha?"

"Nowhere. I just moved into a new apartment."

"Could you be moving on from your relationship?"

"I've thought about it. But I don't want to. Is that what you are telling me, to drop this thing with Larry?"

"No, not at all. I'm just curious about what you're feeling inside your heart. Let's try a game. I'll say 'What I really want is . . .' and then you fill in the blank."

And so flowed Marsha's wish list—a mixed collection of exciting plans, desired objects, and private longings. The Empress was exuding her charm, her enthusiasm, and her ease with expressing her desires.

". . . and a bunch of new houseplants. All of mine are dying right now."

"What I really want is . . .?"

"Well, some new contact lenses—those throwaway kind."

"What I really want is . . .?"

"Happiness. I want to be happy."

"What I really want is . . .?"

"You know, I haven't told anybody this, but I met a guy the other day at Kinko's. He helped me get a paper jam out of the copy machine, and, well, there was a spark."

"What I really want is . . .?"

"And we're going to dinner next Saturday. I haven't told Larry, but . . ."

"What I really want is . . .?"

"I really want to end this thing with Larry. It's a dead-end."

Sure, the cards offered me a hint. But only a hint. And the clue triggered the restaurant image. Fortune-telling does offer clues—there's no doubt about it. But clues lead to more clues that lead to more clues and yada yada yada. Ultimately there's no absolute answer, because life is an open-ended excursion, a process of discovery that keeps revealing itself. Try to fathom what contains or limits the universe and you'll have a pretty good idea about what I'm trying to describe. I mean, is it a brick wall, a stop sign, or a border patrol out there at the edge of space? One revelation leads to yet another revelation. The big climax and answer we're looking for just doesn't exist. But there are clues about how the now is situated. And that's a good place to start.

In short, I assisted Marsha through her *own* divination process. I became a mirroring device. And I did this by asking her question after question after question. When we answer consecutive questions, we start to quell the conscious mind, and it finally relinquishes control, which eventually permits the intuition to go to work and to start delivering latent feelings and hidden truths from within our unconscious. Those are the real answers people are looking for.

I work like this because I refuse to plant anything in my clients' heads. I don't want the responsibility or karma. It's much more effective to let people tell their own story about where they are heading. Marsha was able to hear for herself, with her own voice, where her different conflicts and desires were heading. I couldn't match the detail and poignancy of her own narrative. She told a tale—several, actually—and one of them happened to involve her future. And that's what fortune-telling is really about.

This simplistic, nonglamorous approach was hard-won. In my neophyte days, I tried to offer my clients details and solutions. But people wanted something else, and usually they did something else with the information shared. Often, after a lengthy reading, the caller would back off and close the call with a monologue. It usually went like this: "Yeah, OK, so I hear what you are saying, but let me tell *you* what's really going to happen now." And so they would.

The Mystique of Fortune-Telling

Consider the words *fortune* and *telling*. Let's start with *fortune*. This implies destiny, doesn't it? As Cynthia Giles points out in *The Tarot: Methods, Mastery, and More*, "One's fortune . . . is the unfolding of one's core being; as an individual destiny takes shape, we watch the meaning of a particular life gradually become apparent. It doesn't matter, really, whether you believe life is preordained or made up as we go; in either case fortune sweeps us along on the tides of our own nature."

The "Real" Thing

Telling means "to make known, to express." For me, telling includes myths, fairy stories, jokes, gossip, laundry lists, diatribes, and any other ingenious way I can impersonate the contents of my caller's unconscious. Telling also implies the art of listening, which takes us back to our discussion about divination. Remember your childhood and how a good story impacted your imagination? You were transported to another world.

When we hear a myth, have a dream, experience a painting, watch a film, see a stage performance, or read a book or poem, we enter the enchanted world of telling. There is a kind of transmission that takes place. Metaphor is the universal language of the invisible. Through the symbols, characters, and narrative we are given a view of our inner life. Telling helps us find our bearings, see our story, and make sense of the world we live in.

In truth, a wise fortune-teller doesn't *tell* as much as she helps *mirror* our stories, real or imaginary. It might seem like she's a guide, but her true gift is her ability to support our process of self-inquiry. She acts as a witness to the stories we tell, the stories that we know and imagine. Think about it. We all know the truth about ourselves. But how do we *interrupt* ourselves, step back, and evaluate our private world? It's difficult to do this alone. Through mirroring we are able to weave our way through our rationalizations and fabrications and find our way to the truth, to what's real. And experiencing the truth can make us feel as if the future has been revealed, the labyrinth has been exited, the confusion or stalemate has been unwound. And quite often I hear this request during a reading: "Go ahead, just tell me the truth."

The art of fortune-telling brings the art of stories, the magic of dialogue, and the state of divination into high relief. Suddenly we're given the opportunity to explore and objectify the contents of a secret manuscript that has our name written on the cover.

Soul School

Pop quiz! Who are you?

Several years ago during a retreat on the island of Maui, the spiritual teachers gave us this thirty-minute exercise. Students within the group paired up and took turns asking the question "Who are you?" over and over again. Five minutes into the exercise, people were on a roll: "I'm a man. I'm a carpenter. I'm a father with two children. I'm a person who likes fried chicken. I'm an American Indian. I'm a rebellious person." Ten minutes into the exercise, the content of the answers had shifted drastically, and everything became very Nietzschean: "I am strength. I am the hero on his journey. I am the Will to Power." After fifteen minutes, there were protracted gaps between answers. The mind had started to stutter and deplete its array of definitions. After twenty minutes, half of the large group was silent. They no longer had an answer. Their real self had made an appearance. Presence had asserted itself. There wasn't anything to say.

So what do we do when we aren't feeling the presence of our real self? Study, ponder, pay attention, meditate, and inquire, to name a few of our options. Of course, we'll fall asleep again and forget about our real self, but then something will jar us—usually some type of suffering—and then we'll wake up and hop back on the path again, trying to find out more about how to stay awake. It's an endless cycle.

Unlike our Eastern brothers and sisters, Westerners have a naïve notion about awakening, or becoming enlightened. We underestimate the time and effort that's involved with the process. In a Zen school, a student might have a brilliant spiritual insight and decide to share his revelation with his teacher, who may respond with a loud belch. This is the teacher's way of saying, "How nice for you—now, get back to the present moment." Insights come and go, but the now is always miraculous and yet ordinary.

Magic, divination, and fortune-telling, despite their hokey mystique, remain simple tools for grounding ourselves in ordinary reality. And trusting the extraordinariness of the ordinary is what it means to be real.

Really.

13
Pick a Card, Any Card: The Secrets of the Tarot

The real voyage of discovery consists not in seeking new landscapes but in having new eyes.

MARCEL PROUST

The beauty of the tarot is its immediacy. You purchase a deck of cards, bring them home, unwrap the packaging, shuffle the deck, and *boom!* within a few minutes you're transported to another dimension. It's not like staring at a horoscope for hours and wishing you knew what all the little glyphs and squiggles meant. With the tarot you can explore the symbolic realm in a very visceral way. Each picture on a tarot card is like a mega-mystic vitamin that, once ingested, amplifies your intuitive eye and fortifies your imagination.

The tarot is a kind of language—a language of the unconscious and the dream. Like astrology, the tarot is steeped in mythological motifs, but its symbology is much easier to access. This is why becoming familiar with the tarot's pictorial narrative before trying to master an astrological chart is a good strategy. As methods for self-understanding, both systems are interrelated—but with the tarot you can really *play*. The possibilities for fun, both profound and nonsensical, are endless.

Engaging with the tarot is like sitting down with a bowl of popcorn and a kid's illustrated book of fairy tales; within minutes you are chomping away and lost in the story's magical motifs and dramas.

People usually associate the tarot with fortune-telling and trying to predict the future. But the cards offer insights far above figuring out if your grandmother is going to leave you anything in her will. The tarot presents us with a contemplative mirror in which we can—lo and behold—see ourselves, not in the future but in the here and now, which, ultimately, is much more intriguing. And of course, the "here and now" has everything to do with how the "there and then" is going to show up.

When folks call with a quandary, I use the tarot to help them unravel the unconscious patterns and invisible forces that are affecting their current state of mind. The tarot can help me read their mind—not telepathically but photographically. The cards can provide a visual tableaux, a symbolic way of illustrating the moment we are in and where we might be heading.

Hangin' with the Hanged Man

Pam in Florida felt conflicted. She wanted to find a new boyfriend—maybe. The last guy she was with left town after borrowing five hundred dollars and her cat, Thor.

"What's going on with my love life? I feel like joining a convent. There are so many losers out there. But I'm kind of lonely. What should I do?"

I asked her to relax while I shuffled. I'd decided to do a simple past-present-future layout. The first card I drew, representing her past, was the Hanged Man—one of the tarot's most cryptic figures. It shows a man, with a radiant glow around his head, hanging upside down by his left leg from a tree branch. I described the card to Pam and asked her what the image evoked in her imagination.

"Hung up, I guess. A feeling of being stuck. That's what comes to mind."

"Yes, I get that too," I explained. "I think the card represents a desire to start seeing things differently. Imagine how the world would look to you if you were suspended upside down like that from a tree. Wouldn't everything be reversed?"

"Yeah, it would."

"So I can tell that not too long ago you entered a phase where you decided, maybe unconsciously, to start thinking differently about your relationships, not just to men but to the whole world. It's telling that you joked about joining a convent, because this card has a lot to do with spiritual retreat. That glow around the guy's head means that his new way of seeing the world is illuminating. There's a deep shift of consciousness happening—a new attitude that you adopted recently, probably after your boyfriend left town with your money."

The second card I drew, emphasizing Pam's present situation, was the Eight of Swords. It's a grim image depicting a blindfolded woman bound by ropes and standing in a puddle of mud.

"Jeez, that's really charming," Pam offered.

"But doesn't that correspond to your feeling about the present—like you can't really see where you're going, what your options might be? And that feeling of being left in the lurch? I think this card is fitting. On a deeper level, all of those swords surrounding the woman represent your thoughts—your brain working overtime, believing that thinking will solve your situation. But thinking usually means we are trying to tell ourselves what we *should* be doing, and I don't think that's going to work now. The Hanged Man says don't push the river, just listen, watch, and contemplate. Revelation will come, but not in a scheduled way. Your fear of being alone is disturbing the peace and stillness of the Hanged Man's watchful gaze. Both cards show solitary figures. So I think it's appropriate right now that you are spending time alone."

"OK, I can see what you're saying. But I want to know what's next. I'm tired of hanging. I want some progress. If I don't get involved in another relationship, what should I do with myself?"

"Well, except for your agitation, these first two cards don't depict a lot of 'doing.' As I said, the figures are alone, so it's an internal relationship you need—a relationship with yourself. Let's check out the next card to complete the picture."

I flipped over the Ace of Wands.

"Hot diggity! Here's the image, Pam. A luminous hand, holding a very phallic-shaped rod, and it's emerging from a cloud. If you were to take hold of this wand, what would you do with it?"

"Is it like a magic wand or something?"

"Sure, why not? So, what would you do with it?"

"Turn myself into Cindy Crawford?"

"OK, and then what?"

"I think I'd take a trip. Maybe go to New York, see some big-city living."

"Yeah, I think traveling is a good metaphor. New scenery. A new view. Now, if I tie all of these three cards together, here's what I get. Remember the Hanged Man. He's upside down, seeing everything differently, but waiting, just watching. But then the hoodwinked woman, she isn't seeing much of anything. She's locked up in her mind. So the theme here is a vision thing. It's about what will prevail. This Ace represents a breakthrough. The Hanged Man's perspective is going to sink in and deliver the insight you're waiting for. What do you think that phallic aspect in the card is saying?"

"Something to do with men. It's a guy thing."

"Sure. But I'm reading for you right now, a woman. Do you think your change of perspective has to do with getting in touch with your male side? Your strength and power?"

"Sure. Why not? And I think that's why, even though the old feeling comes up to get with a new guy, I'm not that interested. I want to do something for myself. And I like the idea of taking a trip. I haven't had a vacation in five years. It's about time."

Pam went to New York and called me back a month later to share another version of her "story."

Silent Knowledge

Through its pictures, the tarot reflects our pictures back to us. Like astrology, the tarot is a symbolic, mythic language—a language that describes not only the obvious conditions in our life but the hidden, unconscious content as well. When someone calls and begins endlessly describing all of the specifics of their predicament, I'll use the tarot as an interrupting device. The sound of the shuffling cards evokes a trancelike response from the caller. All of the fretting and worry is held in abeyance while the cards rearrange, preparing to tell their story.

And the story, when it's told, is twofold. On the surface is everything that's familiar and obvious: the romantic disappointments, the pending decision that can't be reached, or the loss of courage and faith. But more revealing are the hidden contents of the unconscious—the unspoken, often unseen conditions that keep the caller's predicament locked in place. But the unconscious is much more than just an amalgam of unresolved drives and ambivalent doubts. It's also a reservoir of untapped strengths, skills, and wisdom—the very qualities the caller is hoping to connect with to enlighten their particular quandary.

Plato taught that obtaining knowledge was nothing more than an act of *remembering*. What he meant by this was that each of us retains *inherent* knowledge about everything in life. In *The Power of Silence*, Carlos Castaneda said that his Yaqui Indian guide don Juan calls this wisdom "silent knowledge" and describes it as a quality "that all of us have. . . . Something that has complete mastery, complete knowledge of everything. But it cannot think, therefore, it cannot speak of what it knows."

Similar to "right-brain" thinking, silent knowledge communicates through the intuition and imagination. The "left brain" works in terms of linked ideas and logical analysis. When we are in a "left-brain" mode, we make conclusions based on reasons and facts. But "right-brain" thinking is nonverbal and metaphoric, and it perceives in terms of the whole instead of the part. Silent knowledge works very much the same way.

The tarot can provide a bridge to this inherent understanding. And it does this by amplifying our intuitive perceptions. Or, put another way, contemplating the tarot's imagery helps strengthen our ability to comprehend metaphor. And the metaphorical realm is one of silent knowledge's principal forms of communicating with us. If you spend enough time with the tarot and familiarize yourself with the definitive meaning of the cards, you can enhance your self-awareness, expand your cognitive horizons, and begin to rediscover silent knowledge.

A Little History

It's a cliché among discussions of the tarot to claim that the cards have few if any accurate historical references. But it's true. No one knows where the name *tarot* came from. And historians are hazy about the origins of the first *deck* of tarot cards as well. It is known that the cards were ubiquitous in North Italy during the Renaissance, but only as a card *game*, not as a tool of divination. Their occult or magical significance was not publicly considered until 1781, when Antoine Court de Gébelin, a student of mythology and archaeology, claimed that the cards were actually an ancient Egyptian book, a catalog of pictures created to preserve the knowledge of a vanished culture.

Although de Gébelin's assessment of the tarot wasn't based in fact, his romantic notion of the tarot's origin made a strong impression on the budding metaphysical and occult societies and schools of the early nineteenth century. The tarot we know and use today stems directly from this seminal period in history.

Cutting the Deck

A traditional tarot deck consists of two parts. The first twenty-two cards, called the *major arcana*, are considered the most important—and mysterious. When you lay out these cards in their consecutive order, you are assembling a symbolic path, a pictorial representation of your life (or anyone else's). All of the major archetypes, or universal experiences of human existence, are represented. The woman depicted in the Empress card, for example, lounging on her throne in a lush garden—that's your mother. And the stoic-looking king, the Emperor, sitting in the wilderness—that's your dad. Likewise, significant passages and spiritual initiations are symbolized in the first twenty-two cards. The Tower has everything to do with earthshaking wake-up calls and psychological calamities. And periods of withdrawal and healing are typified by the Hermit. And so it goes.

The remaining fifty-six cards, which mirror our modern-day playing cards, are known as the *lesser arcana*. Those cards illustrate our everyday concerns—making money, taking vacations, making new friends, and going out dancing on Saturday night. Combined, both groups symbolize all the different forces that affect our lives, along with all the events, characters, feelings, and ideas that provide the material of which human life is composed. And this is why the tarot remains so attractive and engaging. When you contemplate the card's different images, you feel connected—there is something charming and very human about the tarot. And yet there is also a mysterious message beneath the familiar comfortability, an allure that draws you deeper, like a friend sitting next to you and preparing to whisper a profound secret in your ear.

The tarot invites active participation. In addition to using the cards for divination, you can also meditate on their symbols or use their pictures to activate your imagination. With time you'll begin to notice how your recognition—your inherent knowledge—will begin to heighten. Consider what Aleister Crowley, one of the tarot's greatest teachers and authors, wrote in his monumental work *The Book of Thoth*: "The Tarot should be learnt as early in life as possible. . . . It should be studied constantly, a daily exercise; for it is universally elastic, and grows in proportion to the use intelligently made of it. Thus it becomes a most ingenious and excellent method of appreciating the whole of Existence."

When you pick up a tarot deck and shuffle the cards, you are enacting a powerful metaphor. Rachel Pollack says, "Any Tarot reading represents a personal pattern emerging from the chaos of possible combinations. . . . By scattering the deck we return it to chaos; when we bring it back together, it carries the new pattern." The shuffling of the cards is representative of how our intellect usually views life—we see the events in our everyday world as mixed up and random, without apparent order or flow. But when we stop the mixing and place the cards down in a particular order, we begin to comprehend symmetry and the interconnectedness between seemingly disparate situations, people, and events. We can see the meaning behind the circumstances in our life through the symbolic nature of the cards. This is a simplified idea about how the tarot works.

Keep in mind that a certain amount of memorization is required with the tarot. There's no way around it. You wouldn't take a road trip to a strange part of the country without having a map along for the ride. Likewise, time and concentration must be applied to develop a relationship with the cards so that you have a sense of where you are going and what the tarot has to offer. It's important to find good source material to study, which I've listed in this book's recommended reading, to help you understand the tarot's underlying occult symbolism. You need to combine your knowledge of the tarot's literal meanings with your personal, intuitive response to the deck. These two qualities, knowledge and intuition, will create a meditative state, the method of appreciation that Crowley referred to.

Despite the fact that there are hundreds of tarot decks on the market, only a few preserve the original intention of their creators. Most of the "postmodern" decks are useless for a student who wants to connect with the definitive meaning that was *originally* instilled into the symbols of the cards. For this reason I recommend that beginners work with the popular Rider-Waite deck, designed in 1910 by Pamela Colman Smith, under the instruction of occultist Arthur Waite.

And one final note. Don't let the requirement for a little study waylay your curiosity. Deciphering the tarot isn't anything like laboring over an algebra equation. The tarot speaks to the child in each of us, that part of our soul which is inquisitive, prefers playing over laboring, and will choose a picture over a bunch of text any old day. Crowley also offered this suggestion: "Do not be chained by the conventions of what others have had to say about the Tarot. It is ours to make and remake as we see fit." The tarot is a wonderful way to have serious fun with your imagination.

14
Celestial Poetry: The Secrets of Astrology

But what really makes us tick can best be ascertained by astrology, because this science (as all sciences must be) is based on truth, the most elusive quality in any person's life.

SYBIL LEEK

"Just tell me everything."

"Everything about what?"

"Everything about me."

When people call me, they want the intrigue quotient of *War and Peace* condensed and delivered within a fifteen-minute narrative—only the story I tell must be theirs. They also want me to pinpoint alternative solutions to their problems in a profound and concise way. A ludicrous request? Not at all. A legitimate consultation can be delivered in a short amount of time. The reading might lack sophistication, but a few revealing insights can present new options for the caller to consider, and options are what most people are seeking.

I'm certain that "What's your sign?" and "Do you want paper or plastic?" are the two most frequently asked questions in America. People might not understand how astrology works, but that doesn't stop them from jumping for the horoscope section in their newspaper each morning—or calling me to find out how the planets are humming on any given day. The zodiac has a special allure within our collective mind-set because its typologies are charming and eerily accurate. With its rich metaphorical vocabulary, astrology can offer us a succinct and direct way to decipher the mysterious narrative of our lives.

Poems, dreams, and human beings. Each contains secrets waiting to be revealed. Essentially, poems and dreams are arrangements of common, everyday words or pictures, magically configured to reveal a special truth, feeling, or intention. An example: Let's say you have a dream one night that the sink in your upstairs bathroom backs up and the water overflows to the bottom level of your house. Because it is *your* dream and came from *your* unconscious, it holds a special message just for you.

Superstitious people who have such a dream might hire a plumber, but I think a dream like that goes much deeper. In classic dream analysis a bathroom can, euphemistically speaking, represent a place we visit to handle very personal matters. Water often corresponds to our feelings, and a clogged sink could mean that you are repressing emotional issues with which you aren't comfortable. When that water leaks to your house's foundation, it might indicate that those feelings, once revealed, are going to affect your stability, your security, the "ground" of your life.

Poems, too, are like dreams. We read the words that comprise the poem, but hidden within the syntax are the poet's feelings and longings and impressions.

Our lives are like a dream or a poem. On the everyday level we attend to our jobs, make and lose money, fall in and out of love, maybe have kids, contemplate aging, struggle with failing health, and then move to Florida—God's waiting room—and prepare for checkout time. The Buddhists have a term for this trajectory—they call it "the meat wheel." I consider this an apt description because often we feel that the repetitive grind of the wheel is all that life has to offer us. And yet, like Peggy Lee, we find ourselves asking, "Is that all there is?" In the middle of our assembly-line existence, we might sense an absence of meaning or feeling of purpose. Astrology can help us understand what this missing element is about. Through an astrological sensibility we can see how we each have a special function or gift to offer the world.

The psychologist and scholar James Hillman terms this our *calling*. When we are consciously connected to our calling, life takes on a richer feeling, a sense of belonging and genuine participation.

The Law of Correspondences, or Nuking Saturn

Recently I was conversing with a caller about her confusing love life. My attention went to the difficult aspects symbolized by the transit of Saturn in her horoscope. We discussed this for a short while and then, when she couldn't listen to another word, she blurted out, "So you mean to tell me if I could send a nuclear missile out to Saturn and blow it up I wouldn't have all of these problems with my boyfriend?"

I paused for a beat and smiled but took her question to heart. Her suggestion was reminiscent of the way many of us consider astrology. The idea that a gigantic rock floating through a particular segment of the zodiac affects life on earth does seem ridiculous. But that's a hard, cold, materialistic view of the universe, a scientific skew that reduces everything to gas and dust. People confuse astrology with the idea of cause and effect. And they frighten themselves in the process. But astrology is a system of correspondences, not influences. An example: You might say, "Venus is passing through Scorpio today and that's why I have a migraine headache." But astrology doesn't work like that. Astrology simply offers you another way to comprehend your headache. From the astrological perspective, Venus moving through Scorpio *and* your pounding cranium are one and the same phenomenon—those events *correspond* to one another. The apparent cause and effect is one singular happening—not because the planets made it happen, but because your discomfort is a microcosmic happening that corresponds to a macrocosmic event. Pretty heady stuff, huh?

Historically speaking, astrology was developed everywhere across the globe, within all cultures, simultaneously. As Dane Rudhyar, the granddaddy of modern astrology, once said, "Astrology was the first human expression of an awareness of order." From the moment we turned our heads skyward and noted the cycles of the moon and planets, the setting and rising of the sun, the science and philosophy of astrology was born.

A Mythic Language

Mars, the god of war. Venus, the goddess of love. Pluto, the hound of Disneyland. Have you noticed how all the different components in astrology are named after mythological creatures and characters? Well, there's a good reason for this. Over time, ancient stargazers observed that the planets, the sun, and the moon—just like people—possess specific characteristics, energies, and essential qualities. So, too, the signs of the zodiac. As a way to define those cosmic properties, astrologers borrowed the pictorial language of myth. Why mythology? Because the essence of each mythological character corresponded to the essence of each heavenly body and zodiacal sign.

Myths are repositories of potent psychological truths. As Jungian astrologer Richard Idemon explains in *Through the Looking Glass*, "The myths we remember and use, and which are so potent for us today, are still with us because they describe universal facets of human nature, regardless of time or place." When you read the story of Jason's pursuit of the golden fleece, you might recognize a saga that could easily be yours or mine. It's an ageless metaphor and describes a quest to gain wisdom by overcoming our inner monsters—the fears that trap us in the boredom of the safe and familiar. So, astrologers use a mythic, pictorial language to describe the unique qualities that each planet and sign represent. It's one of the surest ways to communicate and explain the correspondences, the connections that exists between heavenly and earthly phenomena. Including headaches.

Through the language of symbol, parable, and myth, astrology can tell you much about yourself. An astrologer does this by composing a horoscope for your birth and attempting to unravel its symbols. Technically speaking, a horoscope is an astronomical picture of the solar system at your day, time, and place of birth. But a horoscope is also a symbol, a mandala or map of the human psyche. It's a model of the drives and impulses that make up a person. I like to think of it as a person's poem.

Astrology can help you comprehend your life—what motivates you and drives the calling that is your unique gift. Psychologists try to do this, too, by studying your dreams, fantasies, relationships, and the various conflicts that perplex you. But I believe a good astrologer can get to the heart of the matter much quicker, and I think this is why Carl Jung, Sir Isaac Newton, Thomas Jefferson, and other great thinkers employed astrology in their quest to understand the mystery of human beings. In a letter to Sigmund Freud, Jung wrote, "My evenings are taken up very largely with astrology. I make horoscopic calculations in order to find a clue to the core of psychological truth."

The Core Truth

OK, so we've looked at myths, what a horoscope represents, and why that picture is important; now let's explore how astrology really works—its real secret. Jung once said, in an unintentionally sexist way, "A man's life is characteristic of himself." This explains how your inner world—comprised of your dreams, compulsions, fantasies, fears, and feelings—will attract, like a magnet, similar energies, events, and relationships from the outside world. So what happens in your life is a representation of the same qualities that are inside you. A good astrologer will study your horoscope and help you define your soul's picture. And when you see more clearly what comprises your inner world, you can apply that knowledge toward understanding the way your life progresses.

Identifying Passion

Kathy was calling. She was bored and felt trapped in a job because of her financial responsibilities. (Hey, welcome to America.)

"What sort of work are you doing?" I asked.

"I'm just a dental assistant."

OK, red flag. Kathy's short response spoke volumes and prompted me to consult my astrological charts for her reading. Issues of identity were up, and astrology is the great identifier. Who am I? What am I about? What do I have to offer? Astrology can help with those questions.

The sun at Kathy's birth was in Leo, the moon in Pisces—fire and water signs, respectively. You might call her a "steamy" type—or maybe "wet hot." With this combination of signs there's a disparity between self-absorption (the Leo part) and caring for others (the Pisces part). And here's a secret about Leo. The easy clichés you read about the sign are misleading—they don't address the real story. The classic Leo temperament is misunderstood. Despite Leo's robust strutting and growling, there's a mouse hiding beneath a haystack. Well, actually it's more like a lantern buried in a haystack. Identity is often weak in undeveloped Leos, which means they become easily identified with whatever job or position they gravitate toward. They use their position to define who they are, and ultimately this undermines them.

Leo's drive for self-awareness is the strongest of all the zodiacal signs. "Who am I?" is a resounding question for them. Now, if that question is answered, "I'm just a dental assistant," there are going to be problems. Big ones. An accurate platitude about Leos is their larger-than-life disposition. They never do things in a small way. If they're depressed, it's suicide. If they're happy, they want to leave town and join an "Up with People" revue.

I asked Kathy to tell me more about her job.

"Well, at first I enjoyed the position and the people I was working with. But lately I can't seem to get out of bed in the morning. I feel listless and I'm really bored—not interested in anything. And that's why I'm calling today. What do you see in my future regarding work?" Kathy's voice was soft and timid, detached from her Leonian heart.

I talked a little about her birth sign, which is another way of addressing a person's *birthright*. The position of the sun in our horoscope, the sign it resides in, designates our promise and potential. The sun sign represents the energy that fuels our process of becoming. The solar force is a promise, which is different from the idea that we *already* possesses our sun-sign qualities. We must struggle to integrate and *actualize* the solar potential in our life. An acorn may indeed contain an oak tree, but what force compels the sprouting, the sinking of roots, and the continuous cycle of growth? Apply this metaphor to yourself. It's the solar force—your sun sign—that energizes the path you follow toward the *real* you, not your parents' idea about who you should be, or your minister's, or that of the culture you grew up in. It's just *you*, the self-actualizing you.

The emotional proclivities represented by Kathy's moon in Pisces would provide a key to solving her dissatisfaction. Why? Because the moon points the way to our heart's desire. Now, for a Leo, the heart's desire is an answer, a palpable solution to the "Who am I?" question. We can use the lunar symbol, the gifts that it represents, to follow our deepest longing. A Pisces moon is an empathetic, romantic, and mystical moon. Kathy's sun-and-moon relationship denoted a commanding presence—a philosophical poet or teacher, an artist and spiritual seeker. But a dental assistant? Well, why not? Who's to say you can't hold a job and still fathom the mysteries of self in your spare time? Or compose poetry or music that allows the soul to express its deepest longings? I certainly wasn't going to suggest that she quit her position and make a quest to India. Besides, there was an element of helping others in her career that appealed to the compassionate nature of her Piscean moon.

"Kathy, I'm curious. What do you do in your free time? You know, your hobbies, pastimes, daydreams. Things you do to relax."

"Oh, I enjoy fiction. But not contemporary stuff. More like the classics. I just finished reading *Pride and Prejudice*, and I've recently started on Flaubert's *Madame Bovary*."

If ever there was a classic sun-in-Leo moon-in-Pisces literary character, it was Flaubert's Emma Bovary. Emma's agitated romantic discontent and self-aggrandizement were symptomatic of a thwarted Leo with strong Pisces undertones.

The moon literally mirrors the sun. This same metaphor is at work in our horoscope. Kathy's moon in Pisces found sustenance through literature's imaginal realm. And those fascinating themes offered her clues. The heroine's rebellion against traditional constraints inspired Kathy's Leonian quest for self-expression. I ventured this idea to her.

She laughed. "Are you serious? I'm calling about my job and you're suggesting I keep reading."

"Oh yes, absolutely. Those stories hold your attention because the characters speak to you. You might not literally hear what they are saying, but that's often the case when we are trying to make a change in our life. Our first hints and pointers come from the imaginal world of dreams, fantasies, and seemingly inconsequential pastimes. Make a list of the qualities you admire most in the book's female characters, put the list under your pillow, and sleep on it. That'll be a magical way to have those characters come into full bloom in your life."

"But what about my job? Should I find something new to pursue?"

"Well, maybe. But I don't think hopping to a new job is going to do it for you right now. You need to build a little more steam. Did you know that Leo is a fire sign? And that your moon is in a water sign? What's water and fire going to create?"

She laughed, and I noticed some volume rising in her voice. She was becoming the lioness. "What? So I need to get steamier?"

"Yes, more passion needs to start churning. You could call it steamier. Think about what happens when you feel romantic. Doesn't life take on a different hue when we're in love? The world feels brighter, and we feel lighter, more connected and passionate. I'm suggesting you invest some time and energy into the things you love."

"And then what?"

"Well, you need to wait and see where your interest and passion start to turn. But start with the obvious. You might consider taking a creative-writing class or exploring the history of romantic literature. Those are two areas that your moon in Pisces would revel in."

"You know, I've thought about writing, but I'm afraid I won't be good at it."

"Try it and see. Don't worry about how good you'll *be*, just see what it feels like to put pen to paper *now*. That's all I'm talking about. Just make a gesture and see where it goes from there."

"But what does that have to do with work and making a change?"

"Everything. When passion builds in one area of our life, it enlivens our relationship with everything else. We feel vital, more courageous. And that's a good space to be in when it comes time to make a change. The more you expand and explore outside interests, the more you'll start to see what you are about, outside of your job. And this insight might lead you in a new direction, a new career. We'll see."

Astrology can't point the exact way we should go, but it can help us highlight the different, sometimes contradictory parts of our psyche that want expression. And when more of our nature is expressed, we begin to feel balanced. And when we feel balanced, our pace is more flowing and trusting. We feel relaxed and disposed to follow the promptings of our soul when it whispers in our ear, "This way."

PART THREE
Unplugging

15

Private Numbers: A Summation of Sorts

Before God and the bus driver we are all equal.

GERMAN PROVERB

For aeons, people have been devising ways to speak with people who are elsewhere. It doesn't matter if the desired subject is across town or under a tombstone—dead or alive, people must connect. To do so, humans invented smoke signals, letters, megaphones, prayers, telepathic channeling, sky writing, confessionals, telegraphs, and telephones, to name just a few of the ways we communicate. Most of these devices demonstrate our preference for talking over listening. Especially the telephone—it's constructed to let you know right away which preference rules. Take a look at your phone's receiver. See all of those little holes in the mouthpiece? There must be about a hundred of them. Now look at the earpiece. There's only four or five tiny openings up there. One hundred holes to five holes: We love to talk. Listening can be arduous, and that's why shrinks and telephone psychics are paid so well. Someone has got to lend the proverbial ear.

Because I do so much listening, friends, family, and people on the Internet consider me qualified to answer this question: "Who actually calls telephone psychics?" Of course, I'm just one little node within the giant oracular switchboard, but I do have some statistics. Fortunately, with Virgo highlighted nicely in my horoscope, I've kept notes on each of my 3,287 calls. I'm not a big fan of generalities, but, then again, I love quirky facts. A look at my collection of private numbers should be quite illuminating.

Callers from Venus, Callers from Mars

There's a big disparity in numbers between men and women callers—which doesn't surprise me. Women were the world's first psychics, so they feel compelled to sustain their ancient origins by dipping periodically into the intuitive pool. Also, women tend to be more experimental and open to alternative approaches to problem solving. And I think this explains their ease and the sense of confidence they exude during conversations with psychics.

Questions about health and appearance are important, and if this means calling a psychic at four in the morning to pinpoint the date of an upcoming bad-hair day, they'll do it. And women love to talk about love; not surprisingly, as my topic statistics indicate, nearly 80 percent of my calls center around romance. So it isn't surprising that 78 percent of my calls are from women.

Men tend to be guarded and skeptical when they begin an inquiry about romance. And they usually have a lot of preliminary questions about how astrology works or how cardboard cards foretell the future. They want to mitigate their uncertainty with a scientific understanding of psychic principles. But articulating the power behind a prognosticative tool isn't anything like explaining the way a hydraulic forklift works. I usually acknowledge their question by asking *them* to describe what exactly electricity is and how *it* works. This tactic usually pays off.

Oddly enough, men are much more generous with their time on the phones, going the distance until the warning beep, a signal to both the caller and the psychic that they have a minute more to go before the computer cuts them off. Women tend to keep their consultations shorter. They have their own cache of intuitive impressions and psychic hunches about the issue that prompts their call. So they'll tacitly compare notes and then it's an abrupt, "OK, yeah, yeah. Got it. Thanks. Bye." But the men, once they're relaxed and get on a roll, will elaborate about the intricacies of their emotional life like an amphetamine-driven John Gray.

Which leads to another intriguing fact about reading material. Of all the specific book titles mentioned, Gray's *Men Are from Mars, Women Are from Venus* is the most frequent. This isn't surprising, as the book is beginning its fifth year on the best-seller list. The second-most-alluded-to tome? The Bible.

States of Consciousness

Where are all these seekers calling from? California and New York top the list—as does the Bible-belt region, which means there are a lot of renegade Christians out there. After my first two weeks on the lines, I was surprised to discover the fundamentalists calling in droves. This perplexed me until the day one customer, after a forty-minute consultation, told me, "I'm a religious woman, and when I'm confused and have trouble hearing what God is trying to tell me, I call a psychic."

"Does it work?" I asked her.

"Oh, sure. I talk about my problems, feel better, and then carry on with my day."

When I started to suggest that the four-dollar-per-minute rate was a little high, she interrupted me and blurted out, "No, it's worth every goddamned penny!"

Right behind the phenomenon of gossip, folks want the enchanted, the otherworldly, the mystical, and the religious to influence their lives—and they want that experience *now*. Psychics fill a spiritual vacancy that might be left blank if not for our keypad accessibility. The convenience and immediacy of the phone allows callers to enact a timeless, archetypal urge—namely, our deep need for dialogue with oracles. The mythic background to the modern astrologer, tarot reader, and clairvoyant is connected with the ancient figure of the magician, shaman, and medicine man.

I take this correlation seriously, and I mix the magical and enchanted elements of the consultation with the practical and utilitarian. I promote ways for the callers to connect with the world of spirit in their private lives—hopefully, without repeated calls to psychics. I feel it's important to support the caller's denominational or philosophical orientation. And if they aren't active with their church, synagogue, or ashram, I recommend ways for them to stick their toe back into the ocean of spirit.

Love Links

One of the first network managers to train me for the lines stressed, as she put it, "The cardinal cosmic law: Positivity neutralizes negativity." She repeated this over and over. At the time I didn't think much about this hokey bromide, but I should have taken it as a serious caveat. People don't call psychics to declare joy or exhilaration. Usually they're in a crisis, and it's usually romantic.

Love may have one central theme—the merging of two souls into one symbiotic joy fest—but this affection can go awry in myriad ways. Being mortal myself and not the angelic source of light and vision depicted on the infomercials, I can relate to many of my callers' plights. Ultimately this makes me a very good psychic. I've been there too: disheveled and drunk, chasing my love object down a dark downtown street at 3 A.M. and whining at them, "Come back! Please, let's just give it one more try." If I were a psychic-reading aficionado, that's the exact moment I would have thought, "Go home and pick up the phone and call. You need some divine intervention, some love potion #9."

Fifty-three percent of these callers are married and usually trying to unmarry, while 25 percent are unmarried and trying very hard to date. Loneliness and longing, intrigue and infidelity—love triangles and quadrangles—keep the lines crackling and throwing sparks. The majority of these calls highlight how the heart and genitals can't strike a compromise. And this stalemate precipitates the need for psychic mediation. This requires dexterity on my part, an ability to talk not only to the caller's heart but to their, um, root chakra as well.

Although management advises against discussing sexual themes, that's like asking a farmer not to discuss crops when he's at the grange.

I've become privy to stories of libidinal antics—and gymnastics—appropriate to a retelling of Caligula's heyday in ancient Rome. The anonymous, confession-booth quality of the lines relaxes the caller's censoring instinct to the point where I need to intervene with a firm "Whoooooa, let's save that little tidbit for *Penthouse* magazine's Forum division." Some of the revelations are humorous, others disturbing, but the purgative result of the retelling allows the conversation to dovetail quickly into why the person really called.

"So, you know, I'm seeing another man. Should I tell my husband that I'm cheating?"

"Yes, I think honesty is important."

"But I can't—not now. I don't want to hurt him."

I acquiesce and offer, "You're right."

And then the volume of her voice ups a notch: "But I can't live with the bastard one minute longer!"

Ultimately, these tales of sexual duplicity bring out the Sigmund in me. I'm sympathetic to how daunting the toggle between the security of fidelity and the thrill of infidelity can be. And it's my job to help the callers see their dilemma in a new light. Perhaps I'll use an old, old story to accomplish my aim. Like the story of Oedipus Rex.

When Freud asserted the psychological relevance of the Oedipal myth, he addressed one of the greatest riddles of the human heart. So I paraphrase this "myth" over and over again for callers trapped in what I call "triangular ambivalence."

It's a tricky narrative, because I certainly can't sit here and yack about King Laius and how he banished his son Oedipus because of some old prophet's vision and the son later murdered the old king and then had sex with his mother and finally went mad and blinded himself with a hot poker. But I do share how the Greeks, being so wise, knew how to tell a humdinger of a tale that addressed, among other issues, the infidelity problem. So I'll explain how every young child has an unfettered passion for the parent of the opposite sex coupled with an equally intense rage and fear toward the competition—the *other* parent.

We'll end up talking about how a love triangle is much more hypnotic and exciting than a love duet. And most of my callers understand immediately where the story is going. They can see how stealing a new lover away from the lover's spouse is like finally winning mommy or daddy back from their childhood nemesis.

Acknowledging the taboo of the Oedipus complex relaxes the caller and takes the frantic edge off of their anxiety. Myths remind us of our commonality and humanness, our desire to not feel stranded in the infidelity triangle. For resolution, I'll recommend they visit a marriage counselor, minister, or lawyer. Options, too, create a sense of relief, which, again, is what the caller hoped to find through the consultation.

I'll usually lug out my pat offering toward the end of every romance call. Plato summed it up very nicely by when he declared, "The desire and pursuit of the whole is called love." To paraphrase, this epigram addresses our displaced mystical impulse and how most of us overlay our longing for Spirit onto the perfect dream mate. When I suggested this idea to a woman caller from New York, she replied, "Are you telling me I that I need to get religion instead of a boyfriend?"

"Well, how about making both a goal, and that way if the guy lets you down you'll still have a relationship with God."

"Hmmm," she said, "I've always fantasized about a ménage à trois."

Oh Lord, Won't You Buy Me a Mercedes-Benz...

My least-favorite topic of conversation is money. Thankfully, money issues comprise only 18 percent of my calls. And I bomb out big time in this arena, so callers are usually disappointed and dissuaded when they disconnect. There are too many unemployed and disenfranchised within this group for me to sleep with an easy conscience. And the last thing I want to share with the caller is another debt to juggle.

The problem is powered by our culture's Las Vegas–inspired lottery mentality. Nearly a quarter of my magic-money calls are requests for winning numbers. It's funny how people don't consider the absurdity of their quest. I mean, if I were so gifted, why wouldn't I use my ability to cull jackpot digits and winning odds from the ethers and hightail my *own* butt down to the nearest racetrack?

Instead, here I sit, the quintessential "family-values psychic." In lieu of launching into a commonsense chat, I'll lay out a few cards and immediately explain, "Joe, it's looking bleak. You've got the devitalized voodoo of the Five of Pentacles hovering above your etheric-body's money portal. This means no-go whenever you gamble." I'll conclude with a quick pep talk, offer to recite a prayer for abundance, and if they press me further, study their alternatives for work and ways to increase their financial prospects. And that's usually when they cut me off mid-sentence and hang up.

Beyond the Fringe

How would you react if someone asked you the best way to perform an exorcism on their three-year-old? And what would you recommend to a woman who wants you to generate a fertility vibration to ensure the functioning of her husband's just-installed penile implant? Or try to imagine your response to this conundrum from a recent caller: "What are my chances of landing a promotion if I take an assault rifle to work and threaten my supervisor?"

Well, if you were me, you'd find yourself pearl diving into the deep ocean of metaphors, symbols, prayers, and spells. Because the border is so thin between sincere callers and genuine kooks, conjuring for these requests requires a huge leap of faith on my part. Hanging up isn't an option for me, because once connected, I feel an immediate and protective link toward my callers, and I'll use my compassion to fire my creative engine on their behalf. This approach might seem inappropriate and downright ridiculous to the rational mind, but people aren't dialing from a rational state of mind. They want to connect with someone who will honor their impulse and investigate the fantastic and nonsensical.

And come on, admit it, we each have private rituals, psychological gimmicks, and imaginal devices that we use like talismans to alleviate the uncertainty of life's mysteries and quandaries. It's a vestige from our childhood. Psychologists call these rituals "magical thinking"—but I call them New Age coping mechanisms. When you connect with a psychic, you're afforded a chance to play with and honor your imaginative, magical way of viewing the world. And if the psychic is any good, you might come away from the exchange with practical solutions to your problems. Well, at least with me you would.

So I offer the callers prayers they can use, myths that mirror their story of the moment, and jaunts through the realm of their active imagination, or I'll prognosticate a life-changing meeting with a soul doctor (read psychologist or counselor) for a fated healing. What the caller does with this information after we disconnect is anyone's guess. I just hope for the best.

As for the aforementioned exorcism, the caller and I did a simple exercise using visual regression. I slowly walked her back in time to her own childhood, where she was able to observe herself and her environment and the fear she felt in growing up with a violent father. This process allowed her to see similarities between her child's feelings and her own and how her unresolved issues might be manifesting through her three-year-old.

For the penile implant, I channeled a little bit of sexual healing conjured from Priapus, the god of happy tumescence.

And for the impulsive guy with the gun, well, we took a journey deep into his imagination to explore what life would be like in prison without any female companionship and way too many amorous glances from fellow inmates.

Zodiacal Ticker Tape

What about astrological numbers? Does one sign of the zodiac call more frequently than another? Well, not in any disproportionate amount. The numbers are pretty equal across the board, although the top notch goes to Virgos, while Leos take the bottom rung on my stellar ladder.

I'm surprised with the low ranking of Leos in the zodiacal pileup. Leos may live under the illusion of complete mastery of the universe, but that's never stopped them from consulting prophets and spiritual pundits to make sure their dominion continues to run smoothly.

Virgo is a paradoxical star sign. Yes, they're pragmatic and frugal, but they're also intrigued with the mystical side of life—in a scientific kind of way. Knowledge for a Virgo is like food. They need information to feel secure about how things are running and humming. Unlike Geminis, who love knowledge for knowledge's sake, Virgos apply their wisdom to personal development and improvement. So this might explain their high number of calls. More information, through foreknowledge, means better living.

What intrigued me most about the Leo/Virgo numbers involves *where* the two signs are positioned in the zodiac—and Leo always precedes Virgo. This means that what Leo initiates, Virgo must assume and make literal. Where Leo's purpose involves self-discovery and self-expression, Virgo, as the following sign, must organize and stabilize, finding pragmatic ways to concretize Leo's creations. Because Leo's greatest contribution is "me," the wonder and mystery of "self," it becomes Virgo's function to make sure that "me" has something to do with itself, like a job or constructive mode of operation. Perhaps this zodiacal sequence explains the numbers. Leos can't afford to have their natural exuberance and trust in life colored by outside influences or opinions. And Virgo? Well, Virgos probably need all the help they can get for trying to formulate ways to take that Leonian *joie de vivre* and put it to work.

Style and Culture

The lines are like a cross-cultural magnet, attracting the colorful diversity of this country and yet revealing what's common to all of us. Basically everyone has the same concerns. But it's the colloquial style of each subculture that makes the lines so interesting.

I surf the demographics of this country every day, and I'd estimate that about 40 percent of my callers are Caucasian, 35 percent African American, 15 percent Hispanic, and the remaining, Asian, East Indian, and Native American.

Most of my African American and Hispanic callers are right in there when we connect. As soon as I answer they're raring to go—ready to play—with a minimal amount of testing or probing. It's just "Hi. I'm Yolanda. I'm a Capricorn and I want to know if my boyfriend is banging the booty on that bitch in the red leotards down at our gym."

My skeptical callers—who are, honestly, more often white—require a lot of preliminary digging and primping. I'll say, "How can I help you today?" and it's usually the same hackneyed response: "Well, you're the psychic. You tell me!" Or they'll offer, "Oh, nothing's going on. I was just sitting here reading *Cosmopolitan* and doing my nails and I thought I'd call." But ten minutes later I'm clawing my way out of the mire of details concerning her husband who just ran off with an Avon lady and how their oldest kid set the garage on fire a couple of hours ago and "Will my husband be coming home soon and will I be able to collect any insurance money on the burned-up car?"

End of the Line

As Disney's "It's a Small World After All" theme plays in the background, let's knit together these groundbreaking facts into a tapestry that expresses our collective spirit. Whether we're a Capricorn, Gemini, or Taurus, whether we're dressed in a sari, spandex, or Chanel, our concerns revolve around three subjects: love, money, and the future, and then putting it together, how the future will affect our heart and vocation.

Love, beyond interpersonal relationships and familial ties, reminds us of our divine heritage and moves us toward a reunion with what we sense is absent in our lives. And yet, paradoxically, love, so the mystics say, is the very ground of our being.

Beyond survival, money fuels our creativity and purpose in life. As James Hillman shows us, money "makes the imagination possible in the world. . . . Money holds soul in the vale of the world, in the poetry of the concrete, in touch with the sea of *facts*. . . ."

And the "F" word? Well, the concept of "the future" is God's way of reminding us of our place in the grand scheme of things, of how, despite our efforts to control and maneuver, spirit is running the show. The future is also a wonderful ploy to keep us occupied with philosophy, spirituality, religion, mysticism, and other systems of belief that humble our hubris and support our efforts to connect with a higher source.

Simply put, people call psychics because they are interested in what the exchange has to offer. Which is—surprise!—a chance to talk. And talking, much more than listening, amplifies our narrative—the story we tell about who we are and where we might be heading.

16
Click, Dial Tone

Nothing succeeds like excess.
OSCAR WILDE

The problem started with nocturnal eruptions.

I'd lay my head on the pillow—ready for sleep—and immediately my unconscious would begin replaying the audio aftereffects of my day on the phones, a chain of discursive non sequiturs comprised of my caller's comments and questions—sound bites, phrases, rants and raves. The stream of voices in my head ran like this:

"Do you think I'm pregnant?"

"He's done things I can't accept—like never cleaning the garage."

"She's a psychopath disguised as a split personality."

"The father went to jail right after their baby was born."

"I've had enough chemo and cobalt treatments to light New York City."

"She's a fox dressed in wolf's clothing."

"He has a honey complexion."

"But I can't use contraception because I'll get a yeast infection."

"When he gets high, he thinks with his other head—you know, his dick."

"I'm a Taurus. He's a Virgo. Tell me it's meant to be."

"With tooth and toenail I'll fight this divorce!"

"I just want to get married and be happy."

"Right before our wedding he ran off with a stripper."

"I'm not worried about money 'cause I pray to Jesus."

I couldn't sleep. My partner Alex told me to cut the cord. My mom suggested I get a job. Vedika recommended I switch to phone sex. My conscience was telling me I'd had enough. And Morton, my teacher, was pressing me to reenter the real world. I told him I was going to write a book. Six months later he requested I take a break from our spiritual school. The heat was on.

Most careers offer opportunities for advancement. Not the psychic lines. There's a price for the freedom of setting your own hours and working from home. Namely, no health benefits, job security, or chance for a raise. In fact, when it comes to pay, the networks are notorious for rewarding their stalwart operators with incremental pay *decreases*. You can imagine the loyalty this generates. And so, like other atrophying operators, I jumped from network to network. Always the new situation was going to get better. And always it was the same enervating stasis. In a single year I worked for five different lines. Only one was ethical—the rest I came to label as Satan's Spawn.

Synchronicity can be a bittersweet force. The quirky way events unfold continually surprises me. And I needed some quirkiness. Not only was I losing sleep, but a month later, like a psychosomatic opera singer, my voice began to fail. I also developed a persistent earache. I imagined a brain tumor. I decided to take a break and practice what I preach: a protracted state of divination. I borrowed some money from my mom, concentrated on my writing, and waited to see if Lady Luck would intervene. And she did. Finally, there was a call I was happy to receive. My agent, Sheryl, was on the line. She'd sold the book.

Waxing Philosophically

Perhaps, as the Buddhists proclaim, humankind is simply one collective yearning, embodied in different ploys, plots, and pastimes. And I think it was Shakespeare who said that there are only ten or twelve stories in life—which repeat through various permutations and settings, ad infinitum. After fielding those 3,287 calls, I can vouch for both of these edicts—especially the ad infinitum part.

During dinner recently, someone asked me how I'd sum up my experience on the lines. Goaded by too much wine, I made a cynical crack about scheduling a lobotomy, but then, during the drive home, I ran an attitude check. My sarcasm had belied my heart. I knew better, or at least my philosophical side knew better. So later, when I was alone, I tried to evoke an image that would symbolize my year-long sojourn on the phones. I saw a river. Well, actually it was a river borrowed from Hermann Hesse's novel *Siddhartha*. And it was the perfect metaphor.

Toward the close of Siddhartha's tumultuous spiritual journey, he finds himself on the bank of a flowing river, listening carefully to the cacophonous sounds of the rushing waters. At first, there's only a garble of splashes and swirls, but later, with a sensitive ear, he hears from within the waters a ceaseless mixture of the human sounds of sorrow, laughter, joy, despair, hope, confusion, death, and renewal.

In my analogy, the telephone's electronic currents were my rushing river, and I too became privy to all of the emotions and longings rushing forward from my caller's hopes, fears, and dreams.

As I contemplated this image I began to understand why my friend Vedika, during our first conversation about my new vocation, warned me about hubris. Before answering my first call, I'd maintained distance from people I felt superior to. Jung would have described me as a guy who was "too high up in himself."

But after my repeated involvement with the folks who called, I began to level out, soften, and lose my prejudice. Like a med student working the emergency rooms, I found the stress, exposure, and demand for immediate, heartfelt response to be educational. The compassion I gained was invaluable. And my skills as an intuitive poet and storyteller amplified as well. In the end I felt like Robert Bly with a headset evaluating Marshall McLuhan's vision of America.

My daily excursions into our collective psyche became the equivalent of an alchemical adventure. I discovered gold in the most unlikely places. And my insights grew incrementally—daily—while connecting, conversing, disconnecting, and then contemplating the quizzical nature of human beings.

It's ironic how a book of secrets should conclude with one of the world's oldest clichés, namely, the fact of our commonality as human beings—how we think the same things, want the same things, dream the same things. And yet there's no denying the unique and palpable spirit of our individuality, the essence of which can transmit over a phone line. We're all one—but each distinct. How paradoxical!

And I had some private insights as well. The first involves my gut-level certainty of the above cliché. I've always espoused the "oneness" thing, but now I know it's really true. And the paradox? The great mystery of being human? Well, rather than trying to solve it, I've started to relax and just accept the paradoxical as meaningful and proper, in and of itself. Or as Van Morrison, my favorite musical mystic, says, "It's not why, why, why, why, why, why—it just is."

Appendix
How to Call a Psychic and Not Go Broke

I want this guide to be helpful and informative. But I'm conflicted. It's hard to remain objective while reporting on such a subjective topic. I mean, when it comes to the supernatural, anything goes. One person's conversation with God is another person's impetus to seek psychiatric counsel. So I'll just cut to the chase and announce my standard caveat: Tread carefully. Before you call, think twice, or better yet, sleep on your decision for a night. I realize the temptation is strong. Calling psychics can be fun—and very expensive. And the convenience and anonymity factor of the telephone doubles the allure.

With competition growing, many networks are dropping their old highway-robbery rates to a per-minute charge that won't break your wallet. And yet, if you can circumvent your impulse, you might do better to spend some time and energy finding a reputable intuitive reader, astrologer, tarot specialist, or shaman in your community. Although you'll forgo the convenience of the telephone, a face-to-face ensures your chances of spending money for an exchange that is worth your time. Jumping into the electronic circuitry of a phone-psychic network is a crap shoot.

But if you're still hankering to call, read on.

To Dial, or Not to Dial: That Is the Question

I suggest that you contemplate two important considerations. The first involves you. Why you are calling? What is your impetus? That's simple enough, and we'll talk about it later.

The second involves the slippery maze you'll enter after you've punched those eleven little numbers. Now, you can enter this electronic labyrinth childlike and innocent. Or you can go in like Xena the warrior princess, ready to challenge whoever tweaks your nonsense meter. Ideally, you'll need a little of both approaches to make your consultation worthwhile.

When you call, chances are you will be given a reading. Note the "chances are" qualifier. Connecting into a psychic network is similar to the climax of the old *Let's Make a Deal* television game show. Curtain number one, two, or three. Which will it be? Unfortunately, the computer switchboards are calling the shots.

Obviously, the value of your reading depends on the psychic's authenticity. If you connect with a flake or a fake, you'll find yourself, like Alice, tumbling down a rabbit hole of confusing gibberish and kooky New Age rhetoric. And that's if you're lucky enough to connect with someone with multiple-personality disorder and a good routine cobbled together. You might end up with a boring dolt who will just string you along with inane questions and not even do a dog-and-pony show for you.

Then again, you could land a legitimate reader who is gifted and sensitive to your time-and-money situation. They are out there, and your mission—should you decide to accept it—is to find that psychic. Is it a needle in a haystack? Well, it's not quite that bad. I'd say it's a ratio of 65-to-35, with the qualified psychics falling into the latter category. So the odds aren't bad. They just aren't great.

Battle of the Professionals

Experts like Dr. Hans Holzer aren't so kind with their evaluation of the electronic-oracle phenomenon. As he notes in his slightly staid *Directory of Psychics*, "900-number psychic readings do not perform a useful service any more than 900-number prostitutes and masseuses do although, as P. T. Barnum once stated, 'there is a sucker born every minute.'"

I don't agree with his assessment, because I think sex lines do perform a good service. They help keep the libidinally challenged happy. And as for 900-masseuses, I've never heard of anyone getting rubbed down over a telephone line. But then again, the things some people do with an actual phone—well, never mind. I'm sure Mr. Holzer's intentions are good. And yet, he's never worked as a phone psychic. So who are you going to trust?

The Author Puts His Money Where His Mouth Is

As I said earlier, what qualifies as a satisfying psychic reading varies from exchange to exchange. I tend to be pragmatic and prefer exploring information that can help me in a practical way. Other folks enjoy the more phantasmagorical side of the New Age: discovering messages from guardian angels, conversing with deceased relatives, or having their present-life conditions tell a story about their past-life escapades.

During my year on the phones and through my Web site, I conversed every day with various psychic operators. We'd exchange gossip and details about our techniques and styles. I met people who worked strictly with astrology and the tarot, others who made numerology their forte, and several who were clairvoyant—using only a caller's voice to receive impressions about the past and future.

But when it came time to write this section of the book, I knew I wanted to get some hands-on experience about what it was like to be on the *other* end of the phone line. I made these test calls on a cold morning in October when there was nothing on television and I felt like doing some research to see what my fellow operators were up to. This meant sitting at my desk, eating doughnuts, and thumbing through a pile of magazines in search of my subjects.

This experiment was scary for a couple of reasons—the most obvious being the money thing. As soon as I dialed and the operator connected, I was hyper-aware of the ticking of the clock. I tend to be a tightwad, so this anxiety really drove home my understanding of how most people throw caution and common sense to the wind when they call.

Another factor was what I call the "oracle syndrome"—a deep, instinctual nervousness that's evoked any time we engage with an otherworldly authority. Our rational mind might pooh-pooh this type of exchange, but our unconscious doesn't.

And so I called. And called. The results? Scary. It took some time to eventually hook up with what I considered to be a "qualified psychic." And time on a psychic line is money, so I wasn't happy when my phone bill finally rolled in. But hey, I knew in my heart that my investment was for a good cause: yours! So I'd like to offer, for your perusal, the three types of psychic operators you'll most likely encounter in your quest. I call them the Psycho-Babbler, the Daft Dawdler, and the Good Psychic.

The Psycho-Babbler

I decided to start with a small advertisement in *Rolling Stone*'s classified section. I was intrigued because the ad promoted psychics who were affiliated with a very official-sounding organization. Apparently this network tested their operators by suspending them over boiling pots of oil until they coughed up the dates for upcoming earthquakes on the West Coast. Well, it didn't say that, but the ad copy tried so hard to sound institutional that I just knew I couldn't go wrong. And yet . . .

I was speaking to a reader named Argonon. Now, don't ask me what kind of parents would name their child Argonon. Of course, they didn't—it was a sci-fi pseudonym or the name of a newly discovered chemical element. Argonon had a sonorous voice. But his pitch seemed controlled and forced—sort of like Harvey Feinstein doing a James Earl Jones imitation.

Once we connected, his preamble was stilted and very, very slow. As he stifled a yawn, he asked for my birth date. I gave it to him, and then he moved into what was obviously an astrology script similar to the writing on those sun-sign coffee mugs you see in novelty shops: "You are a sensitive person who likes people. You are sometimes moody but have a good sense of humor when you aren't angry."

I interrupted and said I needed specific information. He asked me to repeat my name, first and last, three times in a row, very slowly, so he could pick up my vibrations and "feel for the light" around my head. I asked him to please not mess up my new hairstyle.

Light having been felt, I reminded him that I wanted to get moving. I didn't have much time: "Jenny Jones is gonna start in five minutes," I warned. Let the reading begin!

Never mind his skill as a psychic, but his syntax resembled a ransom note compiled of cut-and-pasted phrases from a copy of *New Age* magazine. When I asked him what he was sensing about my boyfriend, he said, "I can see a lot of space and light surrounding him. He's a man. And he has a nice smile and a lot of light that is good for his health and his way and love with you is really happening. He is a nice person who wants to work harder and really strive for his love. I get the number 56 coming in. He's doing something right now, something that's keeping him busy."

"This is pitiful—and get your IQ out of my reading," I thought to myself.

"What about his career? He's thinking about signing some important papers. Would his commitment to this company be a good idea?" I asked.

He paused and then went back into babble mode, declaring, "It's important that he talks to you about this for your own thoughts. The color red will be critical."

"Well, we've already talked. I want to know what you are seeing *right now*. Can you tell me that? How does this new prospect look for him?"

"I can see him striving. And he is reading the papers a lot and worrying," he said.

"Yes, I know, I told you that already. But what else? Should he sign the papers?"

Nonplussed, he intoned, "The papers should be checked with a lawyer. And it will be all right."

"Well, what will be all right—the meeting with the lawyer to vouch for the contract or leaving the project altogether?"

"Yes," he said.

I hung up with my eyes bulging and heart pounding. If I hadn't been so angry I would have probably started laughing. Instead, the parsimonious section of me started counting minutes and dollar signs.

The Daft Dawdler

The next call was to a psychic line whose mascot was a man who looked like he was wearing a football helmet woven from the hair of a lapdog. The reader's name was Barb—not Barbina or Barbarella, just plain Barb. I was soothed by this fact. But seconds later my calm plummeted. I could hear kids in the background arguing about ownership of a PowerRanger. This tiff was interrupted by a booming male voice: "Shut up, goddamnit. Mommy's trying to work." I sighed. Barb engaged. The call went like this:

"Your name please."

"Fred."

"How do you spell it?"

"Excuse me?" I nearly started laughing, but then I spelled, "F-R-E-D."

"And your last name?"

I started spelling immediately.

"Can we start the reading?" I asked.

"Well, I can't be rushed through this procedure. It's critical to the warm-up. And I'm required to get all this stuff for the company I work for."

"Well, I don't have a lot of time."

She ignored this and kept talking.

"Your date of birth?"

I gave it to her.

"OK, that's July, and July is the eighth or ninth month?"

"It's the *seventh* month. It comes after June, the sixth month." I imagined her writing this down very slowly.

"Get daddy some corn chips, Jimmy," came a plaintive call from the background. Barb muffled the phone so the pressure of her hand squeaked and whined through the mouthpiece. When she returned I jumped right in and said, "I need some information about my health."

"OK, we can get to that pretty soon, but first, what city are you calling from?"

"Does that really matter?" My question landed like a bead of water on a Teflon skillet. Barb dimly plugged away.

"Seattle," I offered.

"Is that one word or two words?"

"Oh come on! Seattle! Seattle, Washington. Certainly you have heard of Seattle?"

"How do you spell it?" she asked with mind-numbing sincerity.

"S-E-A-T-T-L-E."

"So it's just one word."

"Yes, yes."

"Thank you."

I'd been on the phone for three minutes—about twelve dollars worth of vapid air.

"Can you tell me anything about my health right now?"

"What's your favorite color?"

"What does that have to do with my health?"

"I just need to know for my forms here."

"Forget the frigging forms," I yelled. "Just tell me something about my health."

Barb's voice rose in tandem with my finger going for the disconnect button on my headset. The last thing I heard was, "Well, I'm picking up *a lot* of negative energy! A lot of anger and . . ."

The Good Psychic

Tony was my next psychic. He was an amiable fellow with a pleasant voice. The advertisement for his network promised a real psychic encounter. At this point I needed something real.

After Barb, I cut to the chase and offered my name, date of birth, and the city I was calling from.

I asked him to tell me a little about his psychic qualifications.

"I'm more of what you would call a hypersensitive person," he said. "I'm not really a clairvoyant. I use the tarot and numerology for my readings. I also work privately and do some of the psychic fairs in Cleveland."

I was listening carefully to how he expressed himself more than to what he was saying. He sounded forthright, so I decided to stay on the line.

"Do you have a special issue or situation in your life you'd like to explore this morning?"

"Sure," I said. "I'm curious about a writing project I'm working on. Can you tell me anything about how it'll go?"

"I need you to relax a bit while I shuffle the cards. I'll be working with the Celtic Cross spread, a standard method of laying out the cards for a question."

I relaxed, he shuffled, and out came the cards.

His reading was accurate. The cards highlighted my anxiety about the lengthy process I was about to enter with my book. But more importantly, Tony was able to let me express what had heretofore been hard to articulate. Namely, my doubts about the subject matter. Like any adventurer, I'd kept my fears to myself, not wanting to taint the spirit of my quest. It felt good to get a reality check on my situation. But was the world ready for a book about telephone psychics?

"The cards involving the future show a slow but steady buildup. So patience is going to be important. The whole theme here is about letting go and yet keeping your mind focused on the task at hand."

He suggested I become more diversified with my time.

"With the Emperor dominating your efforts, you tend to push too hard, creating an all-or-nothing situation. That kind of discipline is good, but it will wear you out in the end. Make sure you stay active, exercise, and take breaks when you find yourself bearing down too hard."

The reading was helpful. I'd been given a chance to dialogue with someone who could not only listen but had a knowledgeable command of their tools for divination. I gave Tony an A+.

Inside Secrets

Why is it so expensive to call a psychic? The entire 900-number industry revolves around dispersing and charging for information or entertainment. Ideally you're paying for the exchange and the psychic's expertise. You're also paying for anonymity and convenience, the ease of picking up your phone and dialing from your home or office. Another factor to consider is credit—the time delay between the conversation and the bill. You're also paying for all of the electronic gizmos that circuit your call. I outlined this in chapter 7.

How do I know what number to call? There are literally hundreds of numbers advertised on television and in magazines and newspapers, so unless you've been living on Mars, you shouldn't have any trouble finding a psychic line. Try to use one of the larger psychic networks instead of the companies that advertise with those two- or three-line classified ads. The major networks are usually associated with a parent company that, because of its reputation, needs to remain in good standing with the FCC. This means there's a smaller chance of being scammed.

Although 900 numbers are regulated by federal law, which provides concrete consumer protection, shabby telecommunications operations are always discovering new loopholes to bypass the stringent FCC regulations.

Watch out for psychic lines that utilize these tactics:

- *International numbers that begin with 011 or 809.* Calls of this nature are not required by the FCC to display price disclosures. The cost might be double the normal 900 per-minute rate.
- *The 500 prefix.* This is used legally as a follow-me-anywhere service. This prefix might redirect your call to a high-priced number without your knowledge.
- *10XXX* (X represents any number from 1 to 9). These numbers might redirect your call to an outrageously expensive international number.
- *800 numbers that offer a free psychic reading.* I've found these 800-number arrangements to be extremely devious. The call is usually answered with a rushed, barely audible prerecorded message that blurts out something like "$1.90 a day billed monthly." Then it taunts you with the promise of a free psychic

reading if you leave your name and a mailbox-service request on the company's answering machine. You are automatically requesting a $58-per-month addition to your phone bill.

I'm ready to call. Now what? First, stop and consider, from a psychological point of view, that you're about to invite a numinous or supernatural event into your life. Although your conscious mind might rationalize and make light of the call, your subconscious will take the exchange very seriously. This is my strongest caveat about calling a telephone psychic. It can be unproductive and sometimes dangerous to have information planted in your unconscious. The unconscious is volatile, and it doesn't miss a beat. It's like a sponge taking everything in and releasing very little.

Human beings are complex creatures. We're a constantly shifting mixture of rationality and fantasy—part child and part adult. And it's usually the child in a person who picks up the phone and connects with a psychic—despite those "over 18 years of age" disclaimers. So while the kid is dialing, the adult's brain is rationalizing, "Oh, this'll be interesting. I'll just do this as a whim." But their childlike imagination is running full throttle, projecting hope and wishful thinking into the world of magic. A seasoned and compassionate psychic understands this situation and handles it accordingly. A successful reading will address the playful, imaginative side of the child as well as the adult's capacity to apply the information and insights that were explored.

What should I consider before actually calling the psychic line? First and foremost, know why you are calling. In other words, spend some time with yourself before you dial. I suggest meditating for about ten minutes on your particular issue or question.

People underestimate the power of formulating a clear question. The more detailed the question, the more detailed your exploration can be. Instead of asking, "When will I start making more money?" go deeper. You might ask, "What do I need to be aware of in my life that would help me start to make more money?" Or "What are the unconscious types of resistance I have to living with more prosperity?"

If you spend a little time beforehand and gain a good sense of what it is you want to investigate with the psychic, you'll feel more relaxed during the call. You'll also be able to know when to disconnect should you meet up with someone who is giving you the runaround. Trust your own psychic instincts.

If I'm impatient and want the reading to start immediately, should I just say so? Like anything else in life, you don't *get* unless you *give*. So plan on "spending" a short amount of time and money to gather some impressions about the psychic. This means listening to them. Pay attention to their voice. The voice doesn't lie. Are they burned out and weary? Or worse, stoned or drunk? Are they snappy and sarcastic? Are they yawning a lot? Is *General Hospital* blaring in the background?

Ask questions about the type of readings they offer. Find out how long they have been working as a psychic and how they developed their skill. Although their response might not mean much to your conscious mind, the instinctual or intuitive part of your nature can tune in like radar to determine if the psychic is sincere. Trust these impressions. And then get on with the reading.

Should I allow myself to be put on hold, participate in a mutual "prayer," or linger while the psychic goes into a meditative state or reads a disclaimer to me? No.

Should I have a clock nearby to time the reading? Yes, but don't watch it. Staring at the clock while the reading is in process will up your anxiety level. Set the alarm on the clock to ring after ten minutes. A good psychic should be able to move toward the heart of the matter within the first five minutes of the reading.

You might offer this information to the psychic. Explain that you plan to be on the line for only a short amount of time, and then stick to your word. Should the reading be rewarding and informative, consider your budget and then continue past your mark. I think a decent reading can take place within fifteen minutes.

Should I expect the psychic to read my mind—to tell me the color of the blouse I'm wearing or what I had for dinner last night? Some individuals working the lines are clairvoyant and capable of performing astounding, Kreskin-like feats—but why waste your money? I think it's better to work with someone who can offer practical information. Some psychics aren't clairvoyant, and yet their skills with various types of divination are sound. Most likely you will meet these types of readers on the phone. Super-gifted clairvoyants usually don't work the psychic lines. So be prepared to be disappointed if you try to run a set of diagnostic tests on your psychic.

Should I offer any information to the psychic at the beginning of the call? If you feel like testing the psychic's veracity, do it tactfully and with good humor. Ask the reader if they can give you a quick, general idea or impression as to what you are calling about. This will prolong your time on the phone, but if it's important for you to determine the psychic's reliabity and sincerity, go ahead and ask. But don't challenge them or throw a defensive attitude. Although the psychic will most likely continue to work with you, their spirit may be daunted if they feel you are skeptical or cynical, and this will taint your call experience.

I'm having financial troubles. Should I still call the psychic line to see if my luck is going to change soon? If you're broke, hocking household items, on welfare, in credit-card debt, or trying to get out of debt, don't call the psychic lines. I know the temptation is strong, because we all like to think that some unexpected turn of luck could rearrange our financial situation, but get real. What are the chances of winning the lottery or a relative keeling over any time soon and leaving you a fortune? Like a painkiller, a conversation with a psychic might temporarily assuage your anxiety, but remember that a fifteen-minute chat is going to cost you around sixty bucks. You don't need the added grief when your phone bill rolls around.

Should I add my name, address, and telephone number to a psychic-networks mailing list? No. Psychic lines are notorious for selling and then reselling their mailing and phone lists to every goofy direct-mail outfit known to humankind. Within a month your address and phone number will have been forwarded to dozens of databases across the nation.

Should you decide to forgo my advice, you'll soon find yourself carting a wheelbarrow out to your mailbox every day to help unload all of the postcards, newsletters, flyers, and bogus sweepstakes offers that will clog your mailbox—not to mention the stream of phone calls you'll receive from both human and automated solicitation services. Worse, your requests to be removed from the mailing lists will most likely be ignored. Also be aware that some psychic lines, once you have called and spoken to a psychic, will pester you almost daily with phone calls to prompt you to call again and again and again. Should you make the mistake of offering your address and phone number to a network—and find that your requests to be removed from the list are ignored—I recommend cutting to the chase and calling the FCC. File a complaint and ask them to assist in your efforts to stop the harassment.

What are your closing thoughts on the subject of telephone psychics? I mentioned earlier that paranormal activities don't mesh well with commerce. And I'm sticking by that statement. The psychic networks are a money-making business. They are *not* the refuge of loving light and good vibrations depicted in their infomercials. And the operators working the phones—usually as independent contractors—are running their own businesses as well and trying to make a living. This means that the psychics are counting on the calls lasting and going the distance. Not only do they need the money, but they're usually working under pressure from the network to *keep you on the phone* in order to make more money. So temper your enthusiasm with a little reality check. If you really feel like calling, go ahead and give it a shot, but keep the call short and to the point. You'll be glad you did when the mail carrier delivers your phone bill.

Recommended Reading

Assuming that many of you are novices or neophites, I've compiled a list of recommended reading material for beginners. Keep in mind that there are literally thousands of books on metaphysics and spirituality at your disposal. This list only nicks the top of the iceberg—although I think it's a worthwhile nick.

Astrology

I experienced quite a shock when I went through my bookshelf trying to find three or four really good astrology books to recommend to a novice. Why? Because I realized how many terrible tomes have been published on the subject. For the most part, authors just regurgitate over and over what other astrologers have written on the subject—and if you've ever played the old game of Telephone, you'll recall how garbled the final "message" can become. I also discovered that my list of "good books" were all written by the same people, so I'll make mention of a few titles and offer my guarantee that any other titles you find by these authors will also be worthwhile.

Liz Greene. *Astrology for Lovers*. York Beach, Maine: Samuel Weiser, 1986.

I know, the title is sort of corny, but as an instructor I always make sure my beginning students purchase this book. Dr. Greene is a Jungian analyst who, along with masters like Dane Rudhyar,

Grant Lewi, and Stephen Arroya, has moved astrology out of the Dark Ages and into the light of contemporary understanding. I don't think I've ever encountered a more straightforward, easy-to-comprehend book on the basics of astrology. It's an absolute must.

Stephen Arroyo. *Astrology, Psychology, and the Four Elements: An Energy Approach to Astrology and Its Use in the Counseling Arts.* Vancouver, Wash.: CRCS Publications, 1975.

Another excellent book for showing how astrology forges a relationship with modern psychology. Arroyo is one of the best.

Grant Lewi. *Heaven Knows What: How to Cast Horoscopes in Just Fifteen Minutes for Anyone Born 1850 to 2050!* 1936. Reprint, St. Paul, Minn.: Llewellyn Publications, 1995.

I carried this book around with me for over fifteen years until, eventually, it fell apart and I had to purchase another copy.

Dane Rudhyar. *The Astrology of Personality.* 1936. Reprint, New York: Doubleday, 1996.

The granddaddy of everything that comprises contemporary astrology. This book really shouldn't be listed as a recommended read for beginners, but it is so comprehensive and amazing that it behooves everyone to add it to their library and then grow into it as their soul matures.

And a final note: If you feel compelled to read sun-sign columns in the newspaper, then you should find and make a habit of syndicated astrologer Rob Brezsny's weekly column, "Real Astrology." His astro-musings are poetic, funny, intelligent, insightful, and he really knows his craft. Most alternative newspapers carry his column. Or you can find him on the Internet at *http://www.realastrology.com.*

Tarot

Arthur Edward Waite. *A Pictorial Key to the Tarot: Being Fragments of a Secret Tradition under the Veil of Divination.* 1910. Reprint, Stamford, Conn.: U.S. Games Systems, 1996.

An erstwhile entry, but formidable nonetheless. I've circumvented a lot of the postmodern tarot books in favor of pointing you in the direction of two of the principal sources, Waite and Aleister Crowley. Waite and the artist Pamela Colman Smith were responsible for creating the first user-friendly tarot deck, the ubiquitous (and rightfully so) Rider-Waite deck. If you have seen a deck of tarot cards or had a reading by a tarot specialist, most likely you've been exposed to the charming medieval illustrations and mysterious symbols that adorn this deck. This was the book that Waite composed to accompany the publication of his tarot deck. Although he's a stuffy writer and sometimes contradictory with his precepts, this book should really be the first exploration you take into the realm of tarot.

Aleister Crowley. *The Book of Thoth: A Short Essay in the Tarot of the Egyptians, Being the Equinox, Volume III, No. V.* 1944. Reprint, Stamford, Conn.: U.S. Games Systems, 1991.

I'll probably get nailed by many of my peers for recommending this book in a beginner's reading list, but the fact is that both Waite and Crowley are the true progenitors of our culture's current tarot revival. Everything that has been written or created as postmodern decks comes after the fact of Waite and Crowley. Yes, this is a difficult book for a beginner to push through, but there are many aspects of the material that remain accessible, especially the divinatory meaning of the cards. In the end, your serious study and concentration will pay off.

Cynthia Elizabeth Giles. *The Tarot: History, Mystery, and Lore.* New York: Simon & Schuster, Fireside, 1992.

———. *The Tarot: Methods, Mastery, and More.* New York: Simon & Schuster, Fireside, 1996.

Amidst the hundreds of contemporary books that have been written on the tarot, these two offer the most concise combination of history, evolution, and modern-day application of the tarot. Although they do not contain the interpretive meanings necessary for working with the cards, they do demonstrate the incredible breadth of various traditions that compile the tarot's history and modern application.

For those with a New Age mind-set, I'd suggest the writings of tarot queen Mary Greer (Newcastle Publishing).

And if you are interested in the more psychospiritual approach to the tarot, I highly recommend Rachel Pollack's two-volume classic, now revised and updated in one volume: *Seventy-Eight Degrees of Wisdom: A Book of Tarot* (London: HarperCollins, Thorsons, 1997).

If you have access to the Internet and Usenet's *alt.tarot*, you won't want to miss one of the tarot's most knowledgeable, practical, funny, and yet curmudgeonly tarot scholars, Jess Karlin. Karlin's commentaries, expositions, and personal Web site are astounding. Why he hasn't written a book on the subject remains one of contemporary time's greatest mysteries.

Philosophical and Soul Studies

As I noted in chapter 12, many of us are aware of our essential self, our inner presence, but we don't know how to approach learning more about it. The following books have offered me a wellspring of insight over the years. And if I were asked to name a series of books that actually changed my life, these books would be dutifully listed. I'm certain they will answer many questions for you about what it means to be a human being living in such a wonderful and mysterious universe, and why we might feel disconnected from the very mystery and beauty that is the ground of our Being.

A. H. Almaas. *Elements of the Real in Man; The Freedom to Be; Being and the Meaning of Life; Indestructible Innocence.* The Diamond Heart Series. Books 1–4. Berkeley, Calif.: Diamond Books, 1988, 1989, 1990, 1997.

———. *Essence: The Diamond Approach to Inner Realization.* York Beach, Maine: Samuel Weiser, 1986.

P. D. Ouspensky. *In Search of the Miraculous: Fragments of an Unknown Teaching.* San Diego, Calif.: Harcourt Brace, Harvest, 1965.

Ramesh S. Balsekar. *Consciousness Speaks: Conversations with Ramesh S. Balsekar.* Redondo Beach, Calif.: Advaita Press, 1992.

Bernadette Roberts. *The Experience of No-Self: A Contemplative Journey*. Revised edition, Albany, N.Y.: State University of New York, 1991.

Christian-Friendly Thought

Marianne Williamson. *A Return to Love: Reflections on the Principles of "A Course in Miracles."* New York: Harper Perennial, 1996.

———. *Illuminata: A Return to Prayer*. New York: Riverhead Books, 1994.

Williamson writes from the perspective of the Christian-based *A Course in Miracles*. For those of you who feel a strong affiliation with this faith, I can't think of two better books to recommend.

Buddhist and Zen Thought

Chögyam Trungpa. *The Myth of Freedom and the Way of Meditation*. Berkeley, Calif.: Shambhala, 1976.

———. *Cutting through Spiritual Materialism*. Berkeley, Calif.: Shambhala, 1973.

I'm a big fan of the Tibbetan Buddhist teacher Chögyam Trungpa. His books are written with a simplistic elegance and grace that inspire as much as they inform. You might need to reread each book a couple of times before the richness of his teaching begins to settle in, but your effort will be rewarded with newfound understanding, freedom, and enthusiasm about your life.

For those intrigued with the principles and deep simplicity of Zen, I've three wonderful books to recommend:

Stephen Mitchell, ed. and trans. *Dropping Ashes on the Buddha: The Teachings of Zen Master Seung Sahn*. New York: Grove Press, 1987.

Charlotte Joko Beck. *Everyday Zen: Love and Work*. San Francisco: Harper & Row, 1989.

Pema Chödrön. *When Things Fall Apart: Heart Advice for Difficult Times*. Boston: Shambhala, 1997.

Alternative Health and Healing

Randy Smith. *Diagnosis Unknown: Our Journey to an Unconventional Cure.* Charlottesville, Va.: Hampton Roads Publishing, 1997.

Often while working the lines I would receive requests for psychic readings pertaining to mysterious health issues that conventional medicine and doctors couldn't seem to cure. In lieu of a metaphysical reading, I would recommend that the caller find a copy of this engaging book.

Psychic Readings and Intuition

Penney Peirce. *The Intuitive Way: A Guide to Living from Inner Wisdom.* Hillsboro, Ore.: Beyond Words Publishing, 1997.

It's ironic, but I haven't really read many books on clairvoyance or telepathic phenomena. These topics don't really interest me. But I do like discovering different ways to foster a *practical* rapport with my intuition, and Penney's book is one of the best.

Psychic-Line Facts and Figures

Robert Mastin. *900 Know-How: How to Succeed with Your Own 900 Number Business.* Newport, R.I.: Aegis Publishing Group, 1996.

For those of you who want a comprehensive picture of the entire 900 telephone business, I can't think of a better book. It really is the bible of an industry that shot from zilch to billions of dollars in annual sales per year.

Want to Work as a Telephone Psychic?

And, last but not least, if you want to find out more information about how to actually land and hold a job as an electronic oracle, you can visit my Web site at *http://zenpop.home.mindspring.com* or send me a stamped, self-addressed envelope at P.O. Box 15414, Seattle, Washington 98115 for further information about my one-of-a-kind report, "How to Work as a Telephone Psychic."

Acknowledgments

It takes a heap of loafing to write a book.
GERTRUDE STEIN

There's nothing to be had from people.
No one will end or begin any stories. There are only friends.
RICKIE LEE JONES

This book's trajectory has been difficult. After a year into this project—and fettered by countless stalls—I became convinced that I must have tortured editors or burned libraries in a previous life. Alas, if my past-life trespasses *are* true, I conclude that karma comes equipped with an escape clause. I found mine through the kind graces of loyal friends, family, and wise business associates (who are now friends). All of which, despite your groaning, will be dutifully listed and acknowledged as follows:

Alex Ellis, for love deluxe and for developing, despite his already generous Libran propensity for bending, a knack for living with a crazed and obsessive Leo rising Six.

Vedika Dietrich—my soul sister supreme—for interminable patience, processing marathons, cogent suggestions, text passages, and beyond-the-call-of-friendship impromptu editing. Your brilliance, humor, and heart make spending time on this planet—and exploring the mysteries of existence—a pure joy.

Morton and Debbie Letofsky, for pearly substances.

My mother, Pat Jones, for making me so mystical; and my father, Woody Woodruff, for making me so analytical. And both of you, for helping fund my endeavors.

My agent and editor, Sheryl Fullerton, an undaunted Aries, for her amazing blend of perspicacity, persistence, and Zen-like patience that demonstrated to me, over and over, an array of different ways to trust in how the universe flows without abdicating one's sense of purpose or will.

Randy and Linda Smith, for a killer title and for kick-starting the vehicle.

Bart Smith, for always believing in whatever I was trying to convince him I was attempting to do despite that fact that I was often clueless as to just what the specifics were—"But it feels like a good idea"—and then asking to borrow money from him anyway. Your friendship and love outshine the northern star.

Bobby Goldstein—the world's best *boychik*—for seeing the word over the paint.

Eric Nord, for your wizardry on a Mac and your stalwart patience and gentlemanly grace through the insane, drive-a-saint-to-drink design process.

Venus "Queenie" Bollig—lots of unconditional L-U-V.

Mique Quenzer—now buzzing in the Absolute—for offering to be the first Harley-Davidson enthusiast trained to work a psychic line. I miss you.

The entire staff at Seattle's Henry Library.

Van Morrison, for his entire musical catalog; and Rhino Records, for their *Soul Hits of the Seventies: Didn't It Blow Your Mind* CD collection—all forty-six disks of which played endlessly in the background while I wrote this book.

Terry and Sheila of the Crystal Psychic Line, for managing their network with intelligence, compassion, fairness, and humor—rare, rare qualities in an industry that's not always governed by the most enlightened practices.

Susan Santomieri, for being my e-mailing, telepsych-kvetching compadre—and one of California's best astrologers.

Cynthia Black and Richard Cohn of Beyond Words Publishing, for pressing the envelope and taking a chance during one of the most paranoid, small-minded, and closed-fisted phases of American publishing history; and Kathy Matthews, also with Beyond Words, for her soothing voice (you should do radio, lady), level-headedness, and insightful feedback that always quelled my doubts (and agitation.)

Gianni (jOnnO) d'Addario, for appearing just when I was beginning to wonder anew.

And, finally, the countless clients and callers who were intrepid enough to broach the numinous world of divination and who trusted in me to assist with their efforts.

Through publishing this book I hope to generate some recognition, verification, and respect for the psychics (phone or otherwise) who continue to practice their vocation despite the hackneyed and inaccurate assumptions that some segments of society hold about their craft. Many of these gifted readers and intuitive counselors are the very wellsprings or channels through which a new renaissance is rushing through our culture. They help create the opportunity and ground for the curious client or student to encounter and explore the object of their quest: a reconnection with the mysterious and secret perceptions that are invisible to our ordinary, one-dimensional mind.

About the Author

Frederick Woodruff lives in Seattle, Washington, and works as a spiritual counselor, utilizing astrology and the tarot in his practice. He also writes regularly on pop culture for various print and online publications. For information about his counseling services or seminar schedules, you may contact him through his Web site at *http://zenpop.home.mindspring.com* or his mailing address at P.O. Box 15414, Seattle, Washington 98115.

Beyond Words Publishing, Inc.

Our corporate mission:

Inspire to Integrity

Our declared values:

We give to all of life as life has given us.

We honor all relationships.

Trust and stewardship are integral to fulfilling dreams.

Collaboration is essential to create miracles.

Creativity and aesthetics nourish the soul.

Unlimited thinking is fundamental.

Living your passion is vital.

Joy and humor open our hearts to growth.

It is important to remind ourselves of love.